IN SEARCH OF
THE ONE

How to Attract the Relationship You've Longed For

Randy Siegel

In Search of The One
How to Attract the Relationship You've Longed For

Copyright © 2016 by Randy Siegel, Asheville, North Carolina, USA

No part of this book may be reproduced in any form or by any means, electronic, mechanical, photocopy, recording or otherwise, except for brief quotations embodied in articles and reviews, without prior written permission of the author.

All rights reserved.

Wyngate Publishing

Printed in the United States of America

ISBN 978-0-9976418-1-3

Praise for
In Search of The One

"Drawing on his personal experience and the wisdom of experts, Randy Siegel leads readers seeking a special romantic relationship toward something even deeper and more profound—a spiritual partnership. Buy *In Search of The One*, absorb its wisdom, and be prepared to attract a relationship so extraordinary that you could only fantasize about it until now."

Shonnie Lavender and Bruce Mulkey
I Do! I Do! The Marriage Vow Workbook

"Siegel, author and beloved relationship coach, has a deft way of seeing you both objectively and subjectively. With near total comprehension, he guides you gently out of what is holding you back and towards the elusive completeness that has been there all along. His personal and honest anecdotes show you how to transcend anxiety and unrealistic expectations. Siegel's own spiritual journey reveals what happens when you stop searching for *the One*, and instead stumble upon *The One*. With touching simplicity, you come away from Siegel's book feeling suddenly embraced by the Higher Power. And also feeling baptized anew by the divine self within."

Elisabeth Shackelford

"*In Search of The One* captivated me from the beginning. Knowing Randy's work for over a decade, this is his best! It is masterfully written from REAL life experiences and just what I needed to read at a pivotal point in my life. Through Randy's innate gift of synthesizing the intellectual, emotional, and spiritual, we are moved into our conscious, authentic, and divine selves and are able to begin living from our true essence. Through a three-path process, our awareness shifts from the 'other' and we learn that in the end, we are the one we long for."

Diane Delafeld

"In his book *In Search of The One*, Randy Siegel challenges one of the great myths of contemporary western society: that we can be made whole by the ideal romantic relationship. Using his own personal journey of deep self-inquiry, Siegel exposes many of the ways our ego mind is constantly engaged in this misguided pursuit. He then urges us to drop to a whole deeper level of understanding, revealing that our true longing is not, as we have been conditioned to believe, for that romantic 'other,' but for the transcendent peace that's intrinsic to our divine self. Finally, he suggests that only after we realize this difference are we truly ready for a mature spiritual relationship. Packed with spiritual practices and simple exercises, Siegel offers a timely and important reminder for those who are seeking true fulfillment in relationship."

Leland Baggett, M.A.
Psychotherapist and Author of Waking Up Together: An Interactive Practice For Couples

"For those disappointed by life, yet who still long—and hold out hope—for a well-matched soul mate, this book is a practicum in taking a beautiful and productive inward journey. Siegel's invitation—to become spiritually healthy and live authentic, transparent lives—guides us down new, un-navigated life paths. While he proffers strengthening our spiritual muscles as a precursor to inviting another into our life, this writer gifts the reader with renewed hope: love can come at any age and circumstance to those willing to fully accept themselves and come to appreciate the special otherness of potential 'ones.'"

Rick McCullough

"Using his own journey of self-awareness, self-discovery, and self-disclosure, Siegel offers a beautiful platform from which he invites us to do the same. He debunks the cultural myths that there is someone or something out there that can save us. Rather, only by knowing ourselves in our most divine essence can we truly be connected, in any significant way, to another. Through practical tools, practices, and exercises, and a treasure trove of wisdom from some of the most influential teachers, writers, and poets throughout millennia, Siegel offers a blueprint to our true selves to help us connect more deeply with what's really going on inside. Timely and relevant, this is Siegel's best book yet."

Cheri Brackett, MA, LPC, ACS

IN SEARCH OF THE ONE

"There are few journeys more confusing and frustrating in this world than the path to Self. And yet, without undertaking this journey we cannot become all we are meant to be, nor share this connected Self with others. Randy Siegel has not only spent time and energy on this journey, he is still there, continuing to seek and find that which he says is most important: The One. Randy is careful to distinguish this search for *The One*—our Divine essence and wholeness, from *the One*—that idealized romantic partner we think will bring joy and healing to our wounded places. Randy shows how moving from the Unconscious to the Conscious Self, from the Defended to the Authentic Self, and from the Higher to the Divine Self brings us to the place where we meet ourselves as we truly know: we are The One we've been waiting for!"

The Reverend DiAnna Ritola

"Randy distills his many years of experience, observation, inner work, reading, and contemplation eloquently in this clear and insightful book. His quest for love and partnership is articulated through deeply spiritual sensibilities. He offers readers a guided approach to living into their innate longing for meaningful connection."

Tayria Ward, Ph.D.

"In sometimes humorous and always heart-felt words, Randy Siegel offers readers three insightful paths and numerous practical steps to unlock our full human potential in life and love. As a teacher and life-long learner, I've already put several of Randy's suggestions to work in my life."

Meredith Tilp

"I love *In Search of The One: How to Attract the Relationships You've Longed For!* Randy Siegel has written a powerful and courageous book that goes right to the heart of one of life's greatest myths. And once he has soothed our minds and eased our anxieties, he goes deeper and not only helps us understand how to find love, but also gives us the steps to do it. Whether you have found 'the one' or are still searching, this is an amazing read that will enhance the relationship you are in or help you find the love you have always wanted."

Meridith Elliott Powell
Business Growth Expert and Award Winning Author

"*In Search of The One* is the book you have longed for—maybe without realizing it. Randy Siegel pioneers an innovative three-path process to guide us step by step to the inner safety, glory, and beauty of our divine nature. Filled with ancient and modern wisdom, *In Search of The One* takes us directly to the heart of this human journey, our soul's longing to express its divinity."

Dr. Christine King
Executive Director, Intentional Wholeness

"This book is a delightful, funny, clear, and concise manual for how to love yourself, love the divine within, and attract the partner for whom you've longed for. It's not just a graduate program for the soul, it's a practical residency program, and if you follow Randy's three paths, you'll experience some of the greatest lessons life has to offer."

— *Rev. Melissa Anne Rogers*
M.Div., MAMFT

"Randy Siegel is so right when he writes: 'There's something seductive about longing.' Ready for change? Grab a coffee, a fresh highlighter, and a mirror. You will not want to put this down."

Sally Spiegel

For Longing
John O'Donohue

Blessed be the longing that brought you here
And quickens your soul with wonder.

May you have the courage to listen to the voice of desire
That disturbs you when you have settled for something safe.

May you have the wisdom to enter generously into your own unease
To discover the new direction your longing wants you to take.

May the forms of your belonging—in love, creativity, and friendship—
Be equal to the grandeur and the call of your soul.

May the one you long for long for you.

May your dreams gradually reveal the destination of your desire.

May a secret Providence guide your thought and nurture your feeling.

May your mind inhabit your life with the sureness with which your body inhabits the world.

May your heart never be haunted by ghost-structures of old damage.

May you come to accept your longing as divine urgency.

May you know the urgency with which God longs for you.

Contents

Section I	**Getting Started**	
One	What You Should Know About This Book	3
Two	Why I Wrote This Book	6
Three	A Bit About This Bozo	7

Section II	**Longing**	
Four	Longing for "the One"	16
Five	Debunk the Myths Around "the One"	19
Six	Stop Savior-Seeking	22
Seven	Could Your Longing Be Misdirected?	24
Eight	Follow Longing Home	26

Section III	**The Three Paths**	
Nine	The Evolution of the Three Selves	32
Ten	The Journey from Ego to Essence	35
Eleven	How to Walk the Three Paths	37

Section IV	**Path One: Unconscious to Conscious Self**	
Twelve	Meet the Unconscious and the Conscious Self	43
Thirteen	The Evolution from the Unconscious to the Conscious Self	46
Fourteen	The Guide: Your Observer Self	48
Fifteen	Chief Obstacle and the Gift	51
Sixteen	Tools, Practices, and Questions	53

Section V	**Path Two: Defended to Authentic Self**	
Seventeen	Meet the Defended Self	62
Eighteen	Meet the Authentic Self	65
Nineteen	The Evolution from the Defended to the Authentic Self	68
Twenty	Make Peace with Pain	70
Twenty-One	Befriend Your Shadow	74
Twenty-Two	Put Your Persona in Perspective	76
Twenty-Three	Burst the Bubble	78
Twenty-Four	Know What Truly Matters	80
Twenty-Five	Express Yourself	82

Twenty-Six	Follow Your Internal GPS	84
Twenty-Seven	The Guide, Chief Obstacle, and Gift	87
Twenty-Eight	Epiphany on Path Two	90
Twenty-Nine	Tools, Practices, and Questions	92

Section VI Path Three: Higher to Divine Self

Thirty	Meet the Higher Self	100
Thirty-One	Meet the Divine Self	103
Thirty-Two	The Evolution from the Higher to the Divine Self	108
Thirty-Three	Place Your Identity on Divinity	110
Thirty-Four	Acknowledge that We Are One	112
Thirty-Five	Be Present	115
Thirty-Six	Relax into Silence and Stillness	117
Thirty-Seven	In Acceptance, Find Peace	120
Thirty-Eight	Welcome Mystery and Ambiguity	122
Thirty-Nine	Become Channels of God's Love	124
Forty	Love, Judgment, and the Unlovable	128
Forty-One	The Guide, Chief Obstacle, and Gift	132
Forty-Two	Enlightenment Is Not a Destination	136
Forty-Three	Tools, Practices, and Questions	141

Section VII Spiritual Partnerships

Forty-Four	Understand Spiritual Partnerships	156
Forty-Five	Commitment	161
Forty-Six	Courage	164
Forty-Seven	Compassion	167
Forty-Eight	Conscious Communication	169
Forty-Nine	Curiosity	171
Fifty	Confrontation	173
Fifty-One	Six Truths about Spiritual Partnerships	176
Fifty-Two	Attract a Spiritual Partner	182
Fifty-Three	Tools, Practices, and Questions	186

Section VIII Wrapping Up

Fifty-Four	Revisit the Highlights	191
Fifty-Five	Poem, Prayer, and Promise	194

Going Deeper	197
About Randy Siegel	201

SECTION I

Getting Started

There is a space between man's imagination and man's attainment that may be traversed by his longing.

Kahlil Gibran, *Sand and Foam*

Hungry for Love

November 1997: As the black BMW pulled out of the lot, I breathed a sigh of relief. Finally, it was over. How could one hour seem like twenty-four? The Internet profile had been intriguing, the computer-driven conversation witty, and the man in the "pic" appeared handsome. Yet once again, I was disappointed. He was a nice guy but not "the One."

Ever since my divorce, I was obsessed with finding the right relationship. I joined organizations, went to bars, cruised hundreds of online profiles, answered ads, and begged friends for introductions. I lived for the blinking red light of my answering machine and checked my voice mail several times an hour to see if the "he of the week" had called. I felt like a bumblebee buzzing from flower to flower only to discover the flowers were artificial. While I met many men who, like me, were lonely, I did not meet a potential partner. As much as I hated to admit it, I thought finding someone special would make me whole, complete my life, and bring me happiness.

I took solace in that I was not alone. My guy and girlfriends seemed to share the same hunger. "I feast on first dates but starve for relationships," one friend complained.

Another friend who was approaching fifty began a rigorous workout routine several years ago. When I asked him about the sudden interest in working out, he confided, "I do not want to grow old alone." My friend felt he had to have an exceptional body if he was ever going to attract a partner.

Fear drives much of our quest for the perfect mate. My own fear drove me to ask a counselor for advice. She told me what I already knew: praying for a partner is useless until I can prepare a place to receive him. Instead of looking for love, time can be more wisely spent identifying the barriers that bar love from my life.

I saw how needy I had become. I dated men who were wounded boys—like me. I had prayed for a savior, someone strong enough to hold me so that I would feel all is safe with the world. Yet I knew the most important relationship I could have was with myself. I needed to learn to hold and love myself. Only then would I be ready for another. I knew all these things, and sometimes I believed them. But all too soon the longing returned. It always returned.

CHAPTER ONE

What You Should Know About This Book

You can employ every strategy out there to find Mr. or Ms. Right, your life partner, or what my friends and I refer to as "the One," but every one of them will fail until you discover the true source of all longing. And if you're like me, what you now think is the true source of your longing is probably not it at all.

While I'm not you, I do have a good idea of what you may be feeling. I've seen this hunger for a significant other too often. Heck I've *lived* it, and it nearly ate me up. I've also found a way to transform this hunger into something that has helped me—and can help you—experience what's been called "the peace that passes all understanding." From there, you'll be ready to attract a conscious, committed, and loving relationship into your life.

I'll explain the true source of all longing and the three paths that will satiate it. Equally important, I'll share that when you make a priority of following these three paths, your intention for being in a romantic partnership shifts from need to spiritual growth. It is at this point that you are ready to attract a relationship so great that you could only imagine it until now.

Perhaps you've read a plethora of books on how to find a romantic partner, and you've seen that the better ones concentrate on the inner rather than the outer world. That makes good sense. First, you have more control over your inner life. Consequently, when you prepare your inner life, you are in a far stronger position to attract that which you seek from the outer world.

Nobody likes a step-by-step foolproof process better than me, but I've found spiritual work doesn't work that way. And as you will see, this is spiritual work of the highest order. There's no one way, and there's no right way. There is only the right way for you. Vietnamese Zen monk Thich Nhat Hanh writes: "All systems of thought are guiding means; there are no absolute truths." Spiritual work is an individual thing, and it follows a spiral path rather than a straight line. If something I write resonates with you, chances are it will be something that you already know or have experienced. But in hearing it again you'll take it down the spiral to a deeper level of understanding and a fuller integration into your life.

Some years ago, a wise teacher told me that I was aware but not awake. By that she meant I understood many spiritual principles but had not yet integrated them into my life. Today, I believe that I am both aware and awake. As you travel the spiral down to deeper understanding, I invite you to seek to integrate those principles that resonate with you in your life. I will show you how.

Writing about spiritual matters is no easy task. For one, we are trying to solve a mystery that perhaps will never be solved. This mystery is beyond explanation; the only way to know it is to experience it. Secondly, the only tools we have available to capture this experience are words, and words are inadequate. At their best, words are vain attempts to describe the indescribable. Finally, writing by its nature is linear, and yet we're talking about a nonlinear process. Bear with me; I'll do my best to explain what I know as clearly, concisely, and with as much compassion as I can.

I will use the term the "divine" a good bit in this book. Feel free to substitute this term with another. Alternative words include: higher power, God, spirit, light, universe, I Am, source, cosmic intelligence, inner guidance, and Christ consciousness. Throughout this book I'll use "The One," with a capital "T," to refer to God or the divine. This is not to be confused with "the One," with a small "t," which I use to refer to a romantic partner.

I'll also include a number of personal stories and examples. As Elizabeth Lesser writes in her wonderful book *The Seeker's Guide: Making Your Life A Spiritual Adventure*: "Writing about the spiritual search without writing about oneself is like writing about a road trip and never mentioning the car."

Throughout this book, we'll examine quite a number of psycho-spiritual concepts. Some I'll present in detail; others I'll provide no more than an introduction. In the back of this book I've included a rather extensive bibliography in case you'd like to explore any of these concepts further.

Some of my thinking is original; some is not. I've been told that I have a gift of distilling, synthesizing, and simplifying information. My hope is that you'll benefit from my years of study. Whether the thinking is mine or from someone much smarter than me, know that all of it has been tested in the laboratory of my life. I have tried to live every word on these pages.

Great teachers don't give answers. Instead, they help people articulate the questions so that they can answer them themselves. Throughout this book I will pose questions to help you frame your own thinking. I've also included several exercises, practices, and tools that I've found valuable in my own journey.

If you are like me, you'll be tempted to skip over both the questions and exercises. You may intend to return to them later. Of course, that's your decision. I've found, however, that when I stop and take the time to answer a question or complete an exercise, I internalize the information in a way I could not have had I skipped over it. I've read enough self-help books to know that insight alone rarely produces lasting change—but practice does. At the very least, I encourage you to take the time to go deeper when you feel particular energy, either positive or negative, around a topic of discussion.

My friend Shonnie, who describes herself as "a parent coach for conscious moms," first taught me how powerful words can be. "Consciously choosing positive words affects our physical, mental, emotional, and spiritual lives," she explained. "Our language creates our reality, so it's important to think about what we communicate." Throughout this book, you'll find a number of lists featuring what I call "power words." If a word resonates with you, I encourage you to write it down in your journal, on an index card, your calendar, or computer file, and make it yours. These power words can serve as inspirational guideposts in our lives. At this moment, my power words include love, acceptance, stillness, and silence. I hope you'll find yours after reading this book.

CHAPTER TWO

Why I Wrote This Book

Authors Flannery O'Connor, Stephen King, and Joan Didion have written that they write to learn. Through their writing, they discover what they believe and how they think. Writing this book has helped me clarify and organize the jumble of thoughts and beliefs that have been in my head and heart, and it's helped me to articulate my spiritual theology and practice.

"As you teach so shall you learn." In other words, what you are teaching is teaching you. This is one of the core principles of *A Course in Miracles,* a collaboration between Helen Shucman and William Thetford. The *Course* is a self-study curriculum intended to bring spiritual transformation. When we teach beliefs and behaviors, as I try to do, we drive those beliefs and behaviors deeper into our DNA. We have to, or we'll appear inauthentic. Readers have built-in BS meters. You know when a writer is not writing from the heart or direct experience.

For years I've read the same stuff as you. "We are one." "You are divine." "You are perfect as you are." "The only relationship that really matters is the one you have with yourself." I said to myself, yeah, yeah, yeah, but I really didn't get the meaning behind these truths. The words simply washed over me. I shrugged them off and went about my day. It's not until I really was able to begin to understand and internalize these concepts that they came alive and had the potential to transform my life.

If you were expecting a guru who can claim enlightenment or who has had amazing spiritual experiences such as speaking with spirits, levitating, or time travel, you'll be disappointed. I'm not that guy. I am a seeker, just like you. But I do have some idea of what you're feeling, and while I don't have all the answers, I've been living with the questions for some time now. Along the way I've learned a few things that I truly believe can change your life for the better and bring you your heart's truest desire—whether you know it or not.

Before we get to that, though, you'll want to have some idea of who is behind the words you now are reading. So here's a brief spiritual autobiography. My intention is to give you some context for all I'm going to be sharing with you.

CHAPTER THREE

A Bit About This Bozo

I've always been attracted to all things spiritual. I grew up in a family that went to church on Sundays. We were Episcopalian, somewhat religious, but certainly not spiritual. Dad was a senior warden of our church, and mother taught Sunday school. She read the Bible to me almost every morning of my childhood, but rarely did we talk about our beliefs, or matters of the heart.

I was an odd child. When other boys were out playing cops and robbers, cowboys and Indians, or Superman, I was in my closet constructing altars and playing priest to an imaginary congregation. My red bathrobe was my vestment. The large gold cross I wore came from my mother's jewelry box; she never knew it was missing.

I also collected crosses. I still do. My house is filled with religious objects, including vestments, chalices, and tiny glass communion cups. Over the years I've had several past life regressions, and in each I served in a religious order. No surprise there.

Looking back over my childhood, I realize my parents were always searching for that something special that I possessed. I felt like a failure because my older brothers were good students, and I was not. I had no interest in sports. I seemed to have little that made me special except for drawing, which I discovered in my junior year in high school. Now at age sixty, I realize that they totally missed the clues: I had a gift for mining the internal.

Even as a young child I had an active inner life. I had an imaginary friend named "Johnny Angel" and felt a connection with the divine that now seems somewhat unusual for a child. I knew from a young age that life was a spiritual journey, and the journey to self and God were related. I understood that life is a classroom and was fascinated with how psychological and spiritual lessons can enrich our lives—if we take them to heart.

In the 1960s, there was a series of popular child psychology books by Dr. Haim Ginott, *Between Parent and Child* and *Between Parent and Teenager*. When my parents purchased them, I couldn't wait to read them. For the next year, I instructed my parents on how Dr. Ginot would handle different situations with me. In my early teens, while other kids were asserting their independence and obsessing over their changing bodies, I was fascinated with the concept of midlife crisis and read all I could on the subject.

Throughout my childhood, I was active in the church. I was an acolyte, soloist in the choir, and founder of a small organization for boys called "The Fellowship of St. Andrew." I attended the Cathedral of St. Philips in Buckhead, an upscale neighborhood in the heart of Atlanta. Sitting through those long services and citing endless prayers—the words of which I did not or could not subscribe to—didn't feel quite right to me. I didn't realize just how un-right this was for me until I went off to Camp Sequoyah in the mountains of Western North Carolina. Here I found a place that could contain my faith. I experienced the divine in rich black soil, cold clear streams and majestic green mountains and was reminded of God through the beauty of creation.

At twenty-four, I considered the priesthood. I met with the bishop of the Atlanta Diocese, a family friend, who encouraged me to go into business and consider the priesthood later. The next year I married, and we joined a downtown Atlanta Episcopal Church where I became active serving on the associate vestry, attending a weekly Bible study, and teaching Sunday school to second graders. I preferred the Sunday early service as it felt more introspective, but in truth I got more from going to workshops and reading psychology books than by attending services.

At age thirty-nine, the world as I knew it crumbled. I admitted to my wife of fourteen years that I was gay, and we divorced. Not only did I come out sexually, but spiritually as well as I left behind organized religion and many of my old "mom and dad values." Two years later I left a big job in public relations, moved from Atlanta to Asheville, and began writing a column, *Confessions of a Late Bloomer*, for men who were gay, married, separated, recently divorced, questioning, or recently out. Over the next three years the column garnered a national following.

About this time I started a new business teaching and coaching professionals in presentation and communication skills. Several years later I developed a model to help professionals package, present, and promote themselves by looking at four Ps: Personhood, Purpose, Persona, and Presence. I wrote a book on this model, *Engineer Your Career: Build Your Best Self Blueprint*, and it became the backbone of my work.

A friend recommended that I attend a weekend gathering outside of Asheville called "Journey Into Wholeness." There I discovered the work of Carl Jung, and this rocked my world. Suddenly I had a language for all that I was thinking, feeling, and experiencing. Suddenly I had a new direction for my life.

Spirituality is the centerpiece of Jung's work. He wrote that not one of his patients over thirty-five was healed until he or she recovered a spiritual orientation to life. I now knew what was missing in my life. I flew to Switzerland to study at the Jung Institute for a short stint, and then found a Jungian analyst in Asheville. I joined a dream group that meets weekly to witness and work with each other's dreams. I heard once that dreams may be our greatest teacher; I believe that.

In addition to all this, I began connecting with the divine through reading, walking in nature, dancing, praying, art, meditating, attending spiritual workshops, journaling, and writing. I found writing to be a form of meditation. Through it, I connect to my own insights and my inner guidance or internal GPS.

Great thinkers, writers, and theologians, including Cynthia Bourgeault, Ken Wilber, John Shelby Spong, and Paul Ferrini, are helping me to re-examine my relationship with Jesus and the church. I currently attend two services in Asheville: one at an alternative church that embraces all religions, and another at an Episcopal church that practices a Celtic candlelight communion. Slowly, I'm beginning to understand my theology.

Below I've listed seven tenets of my faith. As you read them, keep in mind the wise words of American writer and mystic Thomas Merton: "Our idea of God tells us more about ourselves than about Him." By sharing these words, I hope you'll not only get a better idea of my perspective, but also spend a moment or two thinking about your own.

Seven Tenets of My Faith

One: I believe that God is a mystery. It's hard enough—if not impossible—for our small minds to grasp infinity. How then can we possibly grasp the divine that's even more complex and infinite?

Two: My faith is based upon a psycho-spiritual view of God. The more we know of ourselves, the more we know of God.

Three: I believe that heaven is here on earth, and I am in heaven when I am experiencing that "peace that passes all understanding." Love, awareness, acceptance or non-attachment, presence, trust, gratitude, and service help me find this peace.

Four: I believe we are here to individualize and become whole. We've been placed in this big classroom of life, and every person, place, thing, and experience is here to teach us something about ourselves and how to live our best life.

Five: I further believe that all these lessons lead to one basic truth: we are not separate from God. I don't believe that we are God, but I do believe that we are expressions of God.

Six: I believe in a divine order; I believe that everything in our life and everyone who shows up in it are here to help us grow. We are here to remember who we are and to help each other on his or her path. I also believe that there's a big picture; even when times are tough and I can't see it, I can find some peace knowing things are tough for a reason. There's a beautiful Zen saying that comforts me: "The snow falls, each flake in its appropriate place."

Seven: Above all I believe in magic. There's a wonderful quote about magic from Tom Robbins in his book *Another Roadside Attraction*: "Logic only gives man what he needs. Magic gives him what he wants." Even so, it seems the older we get—and the more we may need the magic—the harder it is to believe in it.

My dear friend Beth tells a wonderful story about her soon-to-be-nine-year-old-son. His best friend had found all the presents from Santa in his mom's closet, and he wanted to know if Beth and his father were Santa. Beth took a deep breath and answered yes. When Beth asked if he was disappointed his eyes filled up with tears. "So the tooth fairy is you, too?" he asked. Beth nodded. More tears. They were quiet for a moment.

"I feel like all the magic has just gone out," he said deflated. "There will still be magic," Beth replied. "But it will be different." "But it's not the same," he said.

"No, it's not, but don't give up on the magic," Beth whispered. "There's still magic, whether it's through spirit, angels, possibly fairies, or just the way things happen." Yes, there is magic all around us, and how much richer our lives are when we pause from our overscheduled lives to recognize it.

Magic comes to us in symbols. Yesterday, I glanced out my bedroom window and saw a large black snake slither across the wet, green grass of my backyard into a thicket of hemlocks. I am deathly afraid of snakes, but I couldn't take my eyes off his graceful movement—it was as if it was floating above the grass. My snake had appeared for a reason. Snakes symbolize major transition, transmutation, and even resurrection, and I am in transition. My snake wanted me to stop and appreciate the beauty of this special time. I took in a deep breath and breathed out a prayer of gratitude for the changes taking place in my life.

Magic comes to us in our dreams. When I bought my last house in Atlanta, it was a beautiful yellow stucco bungalow in an in-town neighborhood where I had always wanted to live. It was also my first house as a newly-minted single man. My first night there, I had a dream where I was sliding down the spiral staircase and out the front door. As much as I loved that house, I knew my time in it would be brief. In less than two years I moved to Asheville, North Carolina.

Magic comes to us when we allow the beauty of nature to saturate us. Today, on the way to the gym, I looked out the car window and saw the mountains as if for the first time. Chills went up my spine and once again I was overwhelmed with their beauty.

Magic also comes to us when we believe in something bigger than ourselves. Whether you call it God, the Universe, Higher Power, or the Great Mystery matters not. Life is richer when you believe in something greater than yourself.

Okay, that's enough about me. Let's shift the focus to you. You bought this book for a reason, and the chances are that reason is because you feel like something's missing from your life. Longing: it's a part of our human condition, and it has much to teach us if we're only open to it.

SECTION II

Longing

When I Was The Forest
Meister Eckhart

When I was the stream, when I was the
forest, when I was still the field,
when I was every hoof, foot,
fin, and wing, when I was
the sky
itself,

no one ever asked me did I have a purpose, no one ever
wondered was there anything I might need,
for there was nothing
I could not
love.

It was when I left all we once were that
the agony began, the fear and questions came;
and I wept; I wept. And tears
I had never known
before.
So I returned to the river, I returned to
the mountains. I asked for their hand in marriage again,

I begged—I begged to wed every object
and creature.

And when they accepted,
God was ever present in my arms.
And He did not say,
"Where have you
been?"

For then I knew my soul—every soul—
has always held
Him.

A Six-Word Memoir

I had been looking forward to it all week. The invitation was from a new friend—she invited me (and four other guests) for a simple Sunday supper. She'd provide Caesar salad and paella, and we'd each bring a bottle of red wine or bar of chocolate, along with a six-word memoir.

A six-word memoir? That should be easy, I thought. After all I'm a writer, and in high school I penned many good haikus. Well, I was wrong. Try putting your life down in six words! After several attempts, I came up with one I felt decent about.

The dinner was delicious—my hostess was a wonderful cook. Afterwards we poured another glass of wine and spread the gourmet chocolate bars across the table as we began sharing our mini-memoirs. I began:

"Master of ego; student of soul."

The others followed:

"Kissed a boy; had a baby."

"Started out certain; ended in confusion."

"I had cancer; now I'm clear."

"My mind wanders; like my life."

"Wrote a poem; climbed a tree."

We were having so much fun, we didn't want to stop. We came up with more:

"Yes, I understand; no, I didn't.

"Southern Gothic bride; ran like hell."
"Black white certainty; living in gray."
"Now I know I don't know."

The memoirs came one after another. Then a woman threw one out that caused us all to pause:

"I'm the one I long for."

All of us long to be loved. All of us long for that perfect union with a person we can call our soul mate. And that longing will consume us in a number of unhealthy ways until we:

- Debunk the myths.
- Stop savior seeking.
- Open to the possibility that our longing is misdirected.
- Follow the longing home.

…and ultimately realize that we are the one we long for—or at least a special part of who we are: our divine self. But I'm getting ahead of myself. Let's take a closer look at longing.

CHAPTER FOUR

Longing for "the One"

Whether we are conscious of it or not, longing is a constant companion for most of us. Some experience longing as anxiety, an ache, or sadness. Longing plays softly in the background like a low mechanical hum, the noise of which has become so common that we seldom notice it. For others, longing is more pronounced. At times it becomes so loud that we can hear or think of little else, and an unfortunate few become so resigned to its constant clamor that all hope for peace is abandoned.

For the past six years, I've become a student on longing. I've read hundreds of books, articles, and studies on relationships, attended workshops, and sought the advice of spiritual counselors and trusted friends. And this is what I've learned: all of us long to be loved. We are searching for that perfect love—the perfect union that we read about in romantic novels or see on the silver screen. What we fail to realize is that we are human—and because we are human, we are imperfect. We seek the impossible: perfect love from imperfect people. We fail to see that our longing for unconditional, perfect, or divine love can only be satiated by reunion and communion with the divine.

When our relationships fail to deliver this ideal love, we seek strategies to soothe our sadness. We substitute the desire to be loved with the desire for approval, or to impress and be better than other people. Or we employ a multitude of other strategies to mask our longing, including pleasing, accommodating, and conforming to others' wants, needs, and opinions. In these—and so many other ways—we cry out for love.

Over the years I've had the privilege of mentoring quite a few young people, including two brothers who lived in a large foster care group home twenty minutes outside of Asheville. Twice a month I took the boys for an afternoon outing. Because of the age difference, they lived in separate cottages and rarely got to spend any significant time together. The boys told me that their greatest wish was to find a foster family that would take them both so that they could be together. I can't tell you how happy I was when a lovely couple agreed to take them in. But within six months, the placement failed. The oldest started acting out so much the couple couldn't handle him, and he had to return to the group home. Within months, his younger brother followed and was sent to a different home. I have to wonder if those boys weren't testing their new foster family to see just how much they loved them.

I've found it particularly interesting to learn that the longing for love doesn't necessarily stop when we are partnered. Experiencing what Buddha called the "wanting mind," some of us focus on what we don't have rather than what we do. We compare our partner and relationship to some unrealistic ideal that leaves us restless, listless, and dissatisfied.

Some parents project this longing onto their children. By providing selfless love to their children, they may experience some sort of spiritual connection. But when the kids leave home and are no longer their primary focus, the parents become adrift and unconnected—not only to themselves, but to each other and to the divine. Some of us without children project our longing onto our pets. I've seen many a childless couple treat their animals like divine children, and while they may experience that unconditional love, rarely will a pet fully soothe or satiate their longing.

In his book, *The Eden Project: In Search of the Magical Other*, James Hollis writes that intense yearning has become the chief narcotic of our time. He goes on to suggest that romantic love has replaced institutional religion as the greatest motivational power and influence in our lives. Of course, Hollywood doesn't help. Look at the plethora of happily-ever-after movies such as *When Harry Met Sally*, *Pretty Woman*, and *Cinderella*. Rarely do these flicks draw the connection between romantic love and one's search for the divine. Rather, they carry the implicit message that if your relationship doesn't satiate your longing, meet all your needs, and make you whole and happy, then it's inferior. We've become a culture of longing, and in our romance-obsessed culture, the search for love has replaced the search for God. Our longing for "*the* One" (a romantic partner) has overshadowed our desire for "*The* One" (the divine).

Longing for "the One" is misdirected longing, and we set ourselves up for disillusionment when the object of our longing is another. It's never wise to seek salvation in something or someone outside of ourselves. Confucianism teaches: "What the undeveloped man seeks is outside. What the advanced man seeks is within himself." This type of desperate longing for a romantic relationship is directly related to a separation from ourselves, one another, and the divine.

Like busyness and pleasing others, longing keeps us from being present to ourselves and our lives. We postpone our happiness now for some future event that may or may not happen. Additionally, our longing can thwart a potential relationship. We give off the sour scent of desperation, and since like attracts like, we attract others who are equally desperate. I can remember my first real date after my divorce. He all but ran from the dinner table after the check was paid. Looking back, I don't blame him. I'm sure he felt he had to go home and shower to wash off all my neediness.

Any way you look at it, longing for "the One" is ineffective, unattractive, and even destructive—and yet we continue to long. For one reason, there's something seductive about longing. Perhaps that's why we're so attracted to stories about requited love such as *Romeo and Juliet*, *Les Miserables*, and *The Great Gatsby*. And face it, for some of us the chase is far more appealing than the catch. Like a dog chasing a car, we wouldn't know what to do with a relationship once we got one.

So the message is clear: it's time to wake up, discover the true source of all longing, and change your focus. Whether you found this book or this book found you, get ready to take a closer look at longing, and specifically your longing for "the One."

CHAPTER FIVE

Debunk the Myths Around "the One"

Most of us have crafted a mythology around "the One." Some of these myths come from culture, while others are based upon our hopes and dreams. The first step in waking up is to expose those myths. In my experience, four are particularly prevalent when considering romantic relationships.

Myth One: There is "the One."

I'm a bit embarrassed to admit it, but I used to look across a crowded room, a passing car, or the checkout line at the grocery for my preordained partner. Like in the movies, our eyes would meet, and we would know instantly that the other was the one for whom we had been longing. Consciously or unconsciously, most of us share a similar story. Two-thirds of all Americans believe in the concept of having a soul mate according to a 2010 opinion poll conduced by the Marist Institute of Public Opinion.

Sorry folks, but it's simply not true. Thank heavens! Our odds of finding a happy relationship just went up. Think about it: it's hard enough to find people to date with whom we have common interests, much less common values. It would be so much more difficult if there were only one person suitable for us to partner with for life.

Myth Two: It will be love at first sight.

The popular singles site, Match.com, conducts an annual survey called "Singles in America," in which they survey more than five thousand singles ages 21 to 70-plus. Results from their 2014 survey show that 59 percent of men and 49 percent of women said they believe in love at first sight, and 41 percent of men and 29 percent of women claim they've experienced it. Sorry folks— once again, not true. Lust at first sight, maybe, but not love at first sight. We've got to know someone before we can love that person. And some of the most successful relationships I know began as friendships, including the one I'm in now with my partner Don.

Don and I first met online. I had rented a tiny studio apartment in Washington, D.C. and was splitting my time between there and Asheville, North Carolina. Don lived in Rochester, New York and was renovating a house he bought in Alexandria, Virginia. He loved the D.C. area and hoped to retire there one day. Sparks didn't fly on our first meeting, but we liked each other. And even after I gave up my D.C. apartment, we stayed in touch. Six years later, I was going to D.C. for a board meeting, and I called Don to see if he would join me for dinner. Something shifted during that dinner, and we've been together since.

Myth Three: We will live happily ever after.

In most fairy tales, there's a struggle in which "the One" saves the day and everyone lives happily ever after. The message is clear: all needs, problems, and pain disappear in the arms of love. Put another way, if you're really in love, there's no need to have to work on the relationship. According to psychoanalyst Erich Fromm, love is not a natural act, and it requires patience, practice, dedication, and discipline. Anyone who has been in a long-term relationship knows that's the truth. Pop star Taylor Swift agrees. She's quoted as saying: "I used to believe that you find the one and that's it—nothing's difficult after that. I think that no matter what you find in terms of happiness and compatibility, there's always going to be a struggle attached to it."

Relationships were never intended to magically relieve our pain, heal our wounds, and make us whole. Rather, by walking through the pain, wounding, and longing, we learn, grow, and forge stronger connections with ourselves, each other, and the divine. Like two stones in a rock tumbler, it's the rubbing against one another that creates the smoothest stones.

Myth Four: He (She) will complete me.

Mainstream culture is constantly selling the message that we aren't complete until we are a couple. One of the most memorable lines in the 1996 hit film, "Jerry Maguire" was Jerry's proclamation of love for Dorothy: "You complete me." Comedian Whoopi Goldberg responded years later with her book entitled, *If Someone Says 'You Complete Me,' RUN!* In it, Whoopi tells it like it is in true Whoopi style: "But no one you meet is going to make you complete, a fully realized person. You have to be one before you start any of this relationship shit. Otherwise you're like a goiter attached to somebody, at the whim of how they are feeling."

Incomplete people search for partners to complete them. They enter relationships, and within months or years leave them because they are still unfulfilled. Blaming their partners, they jump from relationship to relationship until it finally dawns on them that they must take responsibility for their own happiness and fulfillment.

Conventional wisdom pictures the perfect couple as two halves that make a whole, but who wants that? Do you want to be a half or a whole? I want to be a whole person in a relationship with another whole person. That's the only way I know to get a whole relationship. "The purpose of a relationship is not to have another who might complete you, but to share your completeness with them," writes Neale Donald Walsch in his book *Conversations with God; Book One*. Ayn Rand puts it in another way in her famous book *The Fountainhead*, "To say 'I love you' you must know first how to say the 'I.'"

These are four of the more common myths around relationships, but there are others including, "He/she will take care of me" and "I'll never be lonely again." These myths compose our concept of fantasy relationships. All of us have one floating around in our imagination. To be in a conscious relationship, we have to let go of these fantasies and the myths that make them up. That can be harder than it sounds, for a part of us—largely unconscious—is afraid that if we give up the fantasy, we also give up the pleasure we associate with the fantasy. Face it: it's fun fantasizing about the perfect relationship. But let's get real. Like a set of faux pearls, real relationships may not appear as fabulous as the fantasy, but their value far exceeds the fake. Real relationships offer us the opportunity to grow, and if we are to grow not only do we have to debunk the myths, we also need to stop seeking a savior.

CHAPTER SIX

Stop Savior-Seeking

Many of us are seeking a savior. We seek "the One" who will save us from our lives and relieve us from our anxiety. We seek, as James Hollis so eloquently writes in his book, *The Eden Project,* "...one person out there who is right for us, will make our lives work, a soul-mate who will repair the ravages of our personal history; one who will be there for us, who will read our minds, know what we want and meet those deepest needs; a good parent who will protect us from suffering and, if we are lucky, spare us the perilous journey of individuation." We look to lovers as gods hoping that they will heal us, save us, and make us whole. We seek white knights to rescue us from the fire-breathing dragons in our lives and by doing so burden them with the impossible—for no one can save us, but us.

To stop savior seeking is no easy task. Hollis writes, "Relinquishing the expectation of rescue by the Other is one of the most difficult projects of our lives."

When I broke up with the first man I lived with after my divorce, one of my biggest fears was what I was going to do when it snowed. My ex was from the North and had no problem negotiating the steep, icy mountain road to our home. I was from Atlanta and was a hopeless mess in bad winter weather. When the first snow of the season hit, I was faced with a choice: I could stay in and wait out the storm, or brave the road. Gritting my teeth, I chose the latter and made it safely out and back home. I'm still not foolish enough to drive when it's icy, but I have learned to navigate the snow—and I have to tell you, it feels pretty darn empowering.

A dear friend of mine had a string of failed relationships, and after a good bit of therapy, she finally got it. She had always sought partners who would provide for her financially instead of focusing on her own career and earning potential. While she was able to attract financially successful men, within time they would become disillusioned with her financial dependence on them and move on leaving her in an emotional and financial pickle. When she shifted her priorities from relationship to career, she was able to build a successful residential real estate practice, and today she's happily enjoying a new kind of relationship—between equals.

We've talked about debunking the myths and how to stop savior seeking. Now we're ready to explore how our longing may be misdirected. Please pay particular attention to this chapter as it presents one of the most important lessons in this book.

CHAPTER SEVEN

Could Your Longing Be Misdirected?

Years ago I had my eye on a used Volkswagen Cabrio convertible. It was white with tan interior. "Should I get it?" I asked the Jungian analyst I was seeing at the time.

"Let me ask you this," he replied. "What does this car symbolize to you?" I thought a moment and answered: "Not caring so much what others think; being creative, free, spontaneous, and not so serious." My analyst paused, allowing my answers to settle and then responded: "Buy the car, or not; it really doesn't matter. But know that these are the things you are truly wanting in your life right now."

His was a lesson I've never forgotten. Whenever I want something, I try to look deeper to see what it is that I am really seeking. What is the reason behind the reason? All of us have missing pieces in our lives, and unfortunately many of us will never complete the puzzle. Why? Because as much as we think we want those things, unconsciously we want something else even more. Bestselling author Debbie Ford called these, "underlying commitments," and unless we bring them to light, we will never realize our deepest wants and needs. Bringing underlying unconscious commitments to consciousness is the first step to regaining your power. "Saying we want things without acknowledging our first commitments in these areas leaves us powerless," Ford wrote in her book *The Right Questions: Ten Essential Questions to Guide You to an Extraordinary Life*.

You may think it's romantic love that you long for, but let me assure you, there's something that you desire more—you just might not know it yet. Sure we want to be loved, but more importantly we want to *feel* loved, and we want to feel loved fully and unconditionally. Unfortunately, in order to find this love we often look outside ourselves. "Imagining others to be the source of love condemns us to wander lost in the desert of hurt, abandonment, and betrayal, where human relationship appears to be hopelessly tragic and flawed," writes author John Welwood in *Perfect Love: Imperfect Relationships*. He continues, "As long as we fixate on what our parents did not give us, or the ways our lover doesn't understand us, we will never become rooted in ourselves and heal the wound of the heart."

We desperately search for "*the* One" when really what we want is "*The* One." We seek the peace and happiness that can only come from reunion and communion with our divine self, and ultimately the divine. You see, within each of us is a deep longing to transcend our feelings of separateness and find within ourselves a new state of consciousness where we feel a part of the whole. We long to return to our true nature—to feel seen, heard, understood, and loved for all we are, or as I am fond of saying, "to stand in our power by becoming the full expression of all we are." And when we become the full expression of all we are, we claim our divinity. As I'll explain later, we place the "I" of our identity on our divine self. But I'm getting ahead of myself.

Previously we discovered that we are unwilling to take responsibility for our own peace and happiness and instead seek saviors to do it for us. To admit that power is within us is frightening. Like Dorothy in *The Wizard of Oz*, we have the power to go home at any instant. But rather than tap our ruby slippers together, all we need to do is simply remember that God is as close as a breath away.

CHAPTER EIGHT

Follow Longing Home

Again, the heart of all longing is the longing for perfect love, for perfect union. Unfortunately we project this longing on a person whom we see as "*the* One," when really what we seek is "*The* One," or union with the divine. By redirecting the object of our longing from "the One" to "The One," our neurotic longing becomes spiritual longing, and spiritual longing becomes the beacon that guides wholeness, connection, peace, and purpose that are the birthrights of our divine self. In short, longing lights the way home to our divine self. Hermann Hesse's character Steppenwolf reminds us, "We have no one to guide us. Our only guide is our homesickness."

Growing up in the 1960s, I lived in a subdivision filled with kids. After school, I was always out in the neighborhood playing with my buddies. When it was time to come home, Mother would ring a bell. If I didn't heed that bell, there was hell to pay! We all have a choice: to heed longing's calling or stick to what we know—what feels safe. If we continue to ignore longing's call, life has a way of presenting challenges until we do listen. I often use the analogy of the "Universal UPS truck driver" to illustrate this point. The driver shows up at the door with a package just for us. He knocks gently, but we choose to ignore his call. The next day he returns and knocks a little louder. Again, we ignore his call. Day after day he returns, and each time he knocks a bit louder. Finally, he has no choice but to drive his truck through our front door.

All of us experience these wake-up calls or "psychic spankings," and too often we choose to turn the other cheek. The divine will get our attention one way or another, whether in the form of a divorce, death, illness, job loss, or midlife crisis. And it's in these times—in the dark soup of the dark night—that we are reborn. Our priorities shift and we begin to pursue the true source of all longing: reunion and communion with the divine.

In her book *Broken Open*, Elizabeth Lesser shares the story of philosopher William James, who wrote that the world is composed of two kinds of people: Once Born and Twice Born. Once Borns stay on the safe, familiar, and comfortable path regardless of what life brings. They stick with what they know and what family and society expect of them. Twice-Born people carve their own paths. Whether through choice or calamity, they make mistakes, suffer losses, and confront that which needs to change within themselves in order to live a more genuine and radiant life. Twice-Born people are aware of the lessons their lives are presenting, and they use the difficult changes in their outer lives to make the harder changes within.

Longing is the beacon that takes us deeper to discover the true object of our longing, and if the longing doesn't get our attention, a life event such as a divorce or death may. When it does, we are called to shift the object of our longing from "the One" to "The One," or reunion, communion, and union with the divine.

In this section, we learned that the true source of all longing is to be seen, heard, understood, and loved for all we are, and that most of us project this longing onto a potential partner. In the next section, we'll learn that by redirecting our focus on three psycho-spiritual paths, we can find peace and grow personally while attracting a special kind of romantic relationship into our lives.

SECTION III

The Three Paths

Journey Home
Rabindranath Tagore

The time that my journey takes is long and the way of it long.

I came out on the chariot of the first gleam of light, and pursued my

voyage through the wildernesses of worlds leaving my track on many a star and planet.

It is the most distant course that comes nearest to thyself,

and that training is the most intricate which leads to the utter simplicity of a tune.

The traveler has to knock at every alien door to come to his own,

and one has to wander through all the outer worlds to reach the innermost shrine at the end.

My eyes strayed far and wide before I shut them and said 'Here art thou!'

The question and the cry 'Oh, where?' melt into tears of a thousand streams and deluge the world with the flood of the assurance 'I am!'

Power in the Pause

After my divorce, I went through a phase of jumping from one relationship to another. "Perhaps you're a serial monogamist," a friend kindly suggested. The pattern would begin when a new boyfriend would move some of his clothes into the spare closet in my bedroom, which would prompt me to ask him to take them home. "I've just become single again," I would explain, "and it's important to me to stay single for a while." He would say he understood and would take his things home. But gradually some clothes and toiletries would reappear. I wouldn't say anything, and before I knew it we were a couple.

At first I rationalized my new status: "I'm simply someone who enjoys being coupled." Later I admitted that I was afraid of being single. Then finally I realized it was something more: I was looking for a partner to complete me. Looking into the eyes of my boyfriend-at-the-time, I reasserted my independence: "I realize that I have fallen into an old pattern," I began. "I jump from one relationship to another, and now I'm feeling a need to be single." He nodded his head. I continued, "I'd still like to see you. I'd just like to cool it off a bit." I scanned his face for a reaction. Nothing. Maybe I needed to be more specific. "I just don't want there to be expectations that we spend every weekend together or see each other exclusively. If one of us wants to see the other, then we should call and schedule a date." Still no reaction. I waited anxiously for his response. The last thing I wanted to do was hurt him. One second… two seconds… three… The silence was agonizing. "That works for me," he finally responded. Whew! I was relieved. At the same time I was a little disappointed. No weeping and wailing? Maybe I'm not such a prize after all. "I need more 'me time' too," he explained. I understood. He had recently taken a new job, moved into a new apartment, and was grieving the recent death of his mother.

Looking back, I now see that this was a pivotal time for me. For the first time I had hit the pause button—I was giving myself time to myself, by myself. I had faced the fear of being single head on. That was progress, and it was the beginning of an intensive period of introspection and growth that I believe paved the way for a spiritual partner to enter my life.

In this section, we'll review the three selves and how the evolution of each can help you on your journey from ego to essence, or your divine self. We'll also introduce the three paths:

Path One: The evolution of the unconscious to the conscious self

Path Two: The evolution of the defended to the authentic self

Path Three: The evolution of the higher self to the divine self

The goal of this section is to provide a framework that will help us delve into a more detailed study of each path in subsequent sections.

CHAPTER NINE

The Evolution of the Three Selves

I wish I could offer you a fast-track to finding the relationship you've always dreamed of, a ten-step process that, once completed, would ensure that you attract the relationship you've always longed for. But I can't. No one can. What I can offer you is a systematic approach that is helping me forge stronger connections with my self, with others, and with the divine. Not only is this approach supporting me to become my best self and live my best life, it's helping me see relationships in a new light: as a means to grow and strengthen my relationship with the divine.

Most of us are splintered into many selves. It's as if we have a gaggle of distinct personalities coexisting within one body that all share one psyche. Montaigne, the French master of the essay, once wrote: "We are all patchwork, and so shapeless and diverse in composition that each piece, each moment, plays its own game." These selves (or sub-personalities, or archetypes) have a purpose: they help us respond differently to different people and circumstances. A few of our many selves may include:

- Teacher
- Student
- Whore
- White Knight
- Distressed Damsel
- Athlete
- Rebel
- Tyrant
- Victim
- Inner Critic
- Idealized Self

Some of these selves play stronger roles in our lives than others; those selves could be called primary selves. Most primary selves were developed in childhood in order to gain approval, or to protect that still-vulnerable child in all of us. One of my primary selves is "The Golden Boy." Psychologists tell us that if we are prevented from expressing our real selves as children, we will then create an idealized self. "The Golden Boy" was my idealized image. When I was able to identify—and even name it—I began taking the first steps to letting my idealized image go. Since then I've experienced a huge sense of freedom as my true authentic self began to emerge.

While it's important to acknowledge and understand our many selves, I've found the evolution of three particularly helpful in living more from essence than ego:

- The Unconscious to the Conscious Self
- The Defended to the Authentic Self
- The Higher to the Divine Self

Each of these three evolutions represents a path. Regardless of who we are—and where we are in our lives—we're already traveling all three paths, whether we're aware of it or not. If we are living, we are evolving—at least to some degree. The more conscious and committed we are to these paths, the faster and further we will travel, and the more meaningful our lives will become.

These paths are neither linear nor systematic. If anything, they spiral, overlap, and intertwine. For a while we might begin working on bringing something from our unconscious into consciousness, while at the same time beginning to shift from defended to authentic self. Then all of that is superseded, because we're shifting from higher to divine self.

Movement toward communication, connection, and communion with the divine requires that we travel three paths at once. Our emotional, mental, and spiritual health depends on it. That said, our gaze may be more strongly directed to one path over the other two at various times in our lives.

Throughout my life I've been on all three paths, but leading up to my divorce, Path One began to take a central role. I started discovering things about myself that were previously unconscious. Of course I came out during that time, but I also began to realize how I had suppressed many emotions, including anger and sadness. Then during and after my divorce, my primary focus shifted to Path Two. I began to learn about many of my defense mechanisms and how each was preventing me from connecting with other people. Now almost twenty-one years after my divorce, my focus has shifted to Path Three. I'm learning much more about who I am and how I can become the full expression of that person. I'm still traveling the other two paths, but my primary emphasis is on strengthening my relationship with the divine.

As each of these selves evolves, we are asked to make a trade—give up something we're attached to that we had believed would bring us peace in exchange for something better. Let's use an experience I had on Path One as an example. I always considered myself a considerate person. But as I got to know my shadow self, I learned that I could also be quite inconsiderate. At first my ego took a small blow, but this insight gave me the option to be both considerate and inconsiderate. I can make a conscious choice about how I want to act, and that's a pretty good trade-off in my book.

Even as we evolve on the first two paths, our ego is not satisfied—it still cries out for "More!" We could be fully conscious about every aspect of ourselves and our lives, and we could be our most authentic self. Yet the ego would not be satisfied—something would feel missing. The ego will never be satiated until we reach the end of Path Three, when we transcend all selves to become divine, or no self. It's here that we find what ultimately we are seeking: "the peace that passes all understanding." It's here that all longing ceases. Even though this experience may be fleeting, once we've found it, we can return over and over again.

Before we examine each of these paths in detail, it may be helpful to back up and take an eagle-eyed view of where these paths lead. Each of the three paths—the unconscious to the conscious self, the defended to the authentic self, and the higher to the divine self—is a journey from ego to essence. Each is an essential strategy for helping us name and claim our essential birthright, our essence, and in doing so attract a special kind of romantic relationship called a "spiritual partnership."

CHAPTER TEN

The Journey from Ego to Essence

You could fill a good-sized library with books written about ego, essence, and how to transcend ego to reclaim essence. My purpose here is only to provide a broad overview in order to place the three paths in context of ego and essence.

There are many ways to define ego. When I use the term ego, I'm not referring to narcissism or self-confidence. I'm talking about ego from a psychological and philosophical perspective. The ego possesses a false sense of self that is composed of the stories we have created about ourselves based upon our perceptions of the past. It's who and what we think we are. Composed of a fixed image of "me, my, myself, and mine," it's what gives us definition in a three-dimensional world, while helping us feel secure and in control in a world that is constantly changing.

Most agree that essence is the most innate fundamental nature of who we are. The Zen masters say it's the "face you had before you were born." And virtually every spiritual tradition teaches that our essence is the presence of God within us. In his book *Beyond Religion: Eight Alternative Paths to the Sacred*, David N. Elkins, Ph.D. shares this beautiful story to illustrate this point:

According to an old Hindu legend, there was once a time when all human beings were gods, but they so abused their divinity that Brahma, the chief god, decided to take it away from them and hide it where it could never be found. Where to hide their divinity was the question. So Brahma called a council of gods to help him decide. "Let's bury it deep in the earth," said the gods. But Brahma answered, "No, that will not do because humans will dig into the earth and find it." Then the gods said, "Let's sink it in the deepest ocean." But Brahma said, "No, not there, for they will learn to dive into the ocean and will find it." Then the gods said, "Let's take it to the top of the highest mountain and hide it there." But once again

Brahma replied, "No, that will not do either, because they will eventually climb every mountain and once again take up their divinity." Then the gods gave up and said, "We do not know where to hide it, because it seems that there is no place on earth or in the sea that human beings will not eventually reach." Brahma thought for a long time and then said, "Here is what we will do. We will hide their divinity in the center of their own being, for humans will never think to look for it there." All the gods agreed that this was the perfect hiding place, and the deed was done.

When we slip into our unconscious, defended—even higher—selves we are operating from the ego. But let's not be tempted to make ego the enemy. In the past the ego had a very basic job to ensure survival. Its tasks ranged from acquiring food and shelter to reproduction. The ego was like a bodyguard whose duty was to protect us and help us feel safe in the world. Today, many of us are less concerned with survival, causing many great teachers to question if the ego has outlived its usefulness. I don't think so.

As long as we reject our ego, we reject an aspect of ourselves and remain inwardly fractured. We'll always have an ego. And as someone who teaches people how to craft powerful personas, I believe we need it to live—and succeed—in the world. It's in our best interest to get to know it and how it operates, so that we can be aware of when, and how, it's at play in our life. When I catch the ego at play, I've found it particularly helpful to ask myself what I'm protecting myself from. In most cases it's a false belief or a fear that no longer applies to my life.

When we move into our conscious, authentic, and divine selves, essence has taken charge. Whether ego or essence is at the wheel is determined by whether we are motivated by fear or love. The ego is motivated by fear, and essence is motivated by love. Fear presents itself in many ways, including confronting, competing, comparing, blaming, judging, striving, worrying, acquiring, deceiving, impressing, self-doubting, withdrawing, manipulating, and justifying. All of these behaviors cause us to constrict.

Essence has only one goal and that's to love. It's committed to unifying and healing so that we can recognize our wholeness or our divinity. When we act out from essence we expand, and it's in this place of expansion and wholeness that we are more likely to attract people—including a romantic partner—into our life.

CHAPTER ELEVEN

How to Walk the Three Paths

In the next three sections, we will cover each path in detail. Each section will include a review of the tasks, guide, chief obstacle, and gift for each path. Like Odysseus in Homer's *Odyssey*, we are challenged to complete tasks along each path of our journey. With the completion of each task, the soul evolves, and it becomes easier for us to choose essence over ego. On each path, we may find ourselves becoming ungrounded. When we lose footing and slip, there's an internal guide waiting to steady us. I believe that we also have many external guides to help us along our way in the form of spirit guides and angels. But these entities can only help us as much as we can help ourselves. We have to call on our inner resources, including these three guides for each path:

Path One: Observer Self

Path Two: Courageous Self

Path Three: Holy Hunger

Again, we'll discuss each of these guides in more detail when we explore each path individually. Right now, my purpose is only to provide an overview.

As we learned earlier, the ego feeds on fear. To protect itself and its interest, the ego will go to almost any length to distract us and keep us hooked into its agenda— including devising seductive enticements along each path. The chief obstacles along each path are:

Path One: Irresponsibility

Path Two: Status Quo

Path Three: Specialness

Finally, each path offers a particular gift that will help us evolve and enhance our lives. Gifts include:

Path One: Choice

Path Two: Connection

Path Three: Peace

Along each path, I'll share various tools, practices, or exercises that may be helpful along your journey. I hope you'll take advantage of these. Insight opens the door, but it's through practice that we actually walk through the door. In reviewing these tools, practices, and exercises, please keep three things in mind:

One: Follow your internal GPS. Follow your energy to ascertain which tools are right for you.

Two: Practice discipline. Discipline is a critical component of any practice. If we're going to progress, we have to put first things first. My partner Don and I recently went on a pilgrimage to see John of God, a gifted healer in South America. During our visit, I met with John of God three times, and each time he gave me a prescription of herbs to take daily. I ended up with enough herbs for six months. As I write this I am still taking them, and while I do he instructed me to abstain from alcohol. I hate to admit that giving up my beloved martinis has been a tough discipline, but it has been also a wonderful reminder of putting what's first, first.

Three: Polish your practice. We've heard it said: "Practice makes perfect." While perfection may be too ambitious, improvement certainly is not. To improve any practice requires:

Intention. Take a minute to explore the goal behind the goal. The goal may be to journal three times a week, but our intention is to learn more about ourselves. Make sure your intention is clear.

Attention. It's easy to get distracted. Instead of checking our e-mail, can we commit to finishing our journal entry? Make the practice a priority.

Repetition. It's said that it takes thirty days to create a habit. Commit to a daily practice for at least thirty days.

At the end of each section I have included some questions for you to consider. I highly recommend that you select those that resonate with you and write about them. If you've never journaled before, I encourage you to try it. Journaling is a simple and effective tool that can help you better understand who you are, how you came to be the way you are, and what direction you should take. Additionally, it:

- Brings clarity to issues in your life;
- Provides a safe outlet to vent pent up emotions;
- Gives dreams and ideas a place to grow;
- Uncovers insights;

- Invites you to deal with your issues honestly in the privacy of your journal;
- Charts your progress.

When you journal, write freely. Some recommend writing by hand rather than on a computer. I do both. Don't worry about smudged ink, spellings, grammar, punctuation, or cross-outs. Your journal is for you and you alone. You may choose to share it with someone later, but when you are writing, write for yourself.

We're now ready to drill down and explore each path in more depth beginning with Path One, the evolution from the unconscious to the conscious self.

SECTION IV

Path One: Unconscious to Conscious Self

Kabir
(English Version by Robert Bly)

Between the conscious and unconscious, the mind has put up a swing:
all earth creatures, even the supernovas, sway between these two trees,
and it never winds down.

Angels, animals, humans, insects by the millions, also the wheeling sun and moon;
Ages go by, and it goes on.

Everything is swinging: heaven, earth, water, fire,
and the secret one slowly growing a body.
Kabir saw that for fifteen seconds, and it made him a servant for life.

Reclaiming the Authentic Self

At eighteen, I enrolled at the University of Georgia at my father's encouragement. He had gone to Georgia Tech, and its large alumni association had served him and his Atlanta business well. During the first quarter, I went through fraternity rush and joined Dad's old fraternity, Pi Kappa Phi. Dad would have been thrilled, but he never knew. He died several weeks after I left for school.

By my second quarter, I had switched from art school to business, declaring a major in marketing. Upon graduation I moved back to my childhood home of Atlanta, took a job in sales, and several years later married a woman whom I would try to shape into my mother. As obvious as it is to me now, it was not then. It wasn't until I turned thirty-eight that I got it: in an attempt to earn my father's approval and love, I was living his life and not my own. What was once unconscious was now conscious, and I could begin the task of reclaiming my authentic self.

In this section we'll meet persona, shadow, open, hidden, blind, and unknown selves. We'll learn that the crucial task for Path One is to know one's self, and you'll discover a helpful guide—the observer or witness self. We'll cover irresponsibility—the chief obstacle on the first path—and choice, the path's gift. Finally, we'll review several practices, exercises, and questions that will assist you on your way.

CHAPTER TWELVE

Meet the Unconscious and the Conscious Selves

The unconscious consists of thoughts, feelings, drives, fantasies, motives, and reactions of which we are unaware, but which influence every aspect of our lives including mental, emotional, interpersonal, sexual, and professional. I read once that the unconscious can influence up to 90 percent of our lives without us even knowing it. The unconscious is a powerful thing. Sigmund Freud certainly thought so. He was the first to place the unconscious at the center of modern psychology. Some people blame the unconscious for every mistake, failure, or unwanted reaction they have while others consider it the magical genie's lamp capable of helping us manifest any desire. Both lines of reasoning carry truth.

The unconscious decides where and how memories are stored, and it may hide certain memories, traumas, and information that we are not prepared to consciously process at this time. When we are ready, they surface so that we can deal with them.

The unconscious is very literal and doesn't process negatives. For example, if you think, "I don't want to criticize my partner," it will focus on criticizing. Let's try it. Don't think about monkeys. Chances are monkeys immediately came to your mind.

Finally, the unconscious thinks in pictures—not words, and it communicates through symbols and emotions. Dreams and the characters that star in them are postcards from the unconscious. By interpreting these symbols and characters, we're able to uncover what's going on in the unconscious mind. Throughout this book I'll share examples of how mining dreams helps bring what is unconscious to consciousness.

The unconscious is composed of what University of California researchers Joseph Luft and Harry Ingham called the blind and unknown selves. Blind self is what we don't know about ourselves and others see; unknown self is what we don't know and others don't see. While for obvious reasons I can't speak to my experience with the unknown self, I can about the blind self. I'm in a dream group, and each week we take turns interpreting each other's dreams. I've noticed that while the message of a dream may be totally clear to the group, it's not at all clear to the dreamer. Sometimes we resist seeing what is obvious to others, especially when it threatens to disrupt our image of ourselves. I've learned to remain open when the group observes something about a dream that doesn't seem to resonate with me. Sometimes—even weeks later—what they've observed will suddenly come into focus.

Now we'll meet the shadow, a prominent inhabitant of the unconscious. And we can't meet the shadow without also meeting its counterpart, the persona.

Meet the Shadow and Persona

Most of us spend the first half of our lives building a defined public image, or persona, only to have to dismantle it in the second half. The persona isn't bad or evil—it's just not totally authentic. The shadow is the flipside of persona—it's the Mr. Hyde to our Dr. Jekyll. The shadow represents those parts of our personalities that we have banished from our personas because we were either punished or made to feel embarrassed for displaying them as a young child.

In his book *On This Journey We Call Our Life: Living the Question*, Jungian analyst and author James Hollis explains how the shadow shows up in our lives: "Where the fears are, is the shadow's dwelling, and it renews its course in our life through sundry disguises such as projection onto others, repression of a vital part of ourselves, or as the narrowing of life—the wearing of shoes too small."

Swiss psychologist Carl Jung believed one of our primary tasks at midlife is to integrate our shadow into awareness. Generally, the more we have cultivated and protected a chosen persona, the more shadow work we need to do. For most of my professional life I had a highly crafted persona, and I was pretty good at protecting and promoting it—so good that I created a career teaching and coaching professionals on how to package, present, and promote themselves.

You may remember that my persona has a name: "The Golden Boy." When I was in my thirties, I bought a 1940s paper mache four-foot tall mannequin of a young boy that had been spray painted gold. I paid way too much for it. It's a relic from the past and a beautiful piece of art, but more importantly to me, it's a symbol of the image I thought I was expected to project.

I grew up in a home where it wasn't okay to be who you are. This may sound familiar to many of you. To garner my parents' approval, I adopted "The Golden Boy," an image that was a combination of Eagle Scout, church acolyte, and the Good Samaritan. "The Golden Boy" has been a part of me for as long as I can remember. When I was ten years old, I was at church with my parents, standing in line at the children's water fountain. Knowing my parents were watching, I stepped aside to allow a younger child to go in front of me. I didn't do it because it was the right thing to do; I did it because I knew my parents were watching and would praise my unselfishness.

In my shadow lurks another self that I call "The Bad Seed." The name comes from my mother who once called me that in a fit of anger. She got it from a horror-thriller movie of the same name that was released the year after I was born. My internal Bad Seed is composed of the part of me that is selfish, inconsiderate, and totally unaware of those around him.

Now that we have some sense of the unconscious self, we are ready to explore its evolution to consciousness.

CHAPTER THIRTEEN

The Evolution from the Unconscious to the Conscious Self

Gnosticism is a philosophical, religious movement that some believe pre-dated Christian times. In ancient Gnostic thinking, Jesus taught that we must be redeemed from our unconscious impulses—not from sin. Sin is the outcome of unconscious states. By learning our true nature, we can awaken to a new way of being in the world.

"Know thyself" was said to have been inscribed at the entry of the sacred oracle in Delphi. "The essence of knowledge is self-knowledge," claimed the Greek philosopher Plato. Centuries before him, the Hindu Upanishads confirmed that "Enquiry into the truth of the Self is knowledge." Centuries later the Persian poet Rumi wondered, "Who am I in the midst of all this thought traffic?" Throughout the ages, sages and philosophers have taught the importance of self-knowledge.

The central task of Path One is to know your self. It's the ability to see how your emotions and perceptions are influencing your thinking and behavior. "No one achieves a full direct view of himself, only the merest glimpse as swift as a thought," writes John O'Donohue in *Beauty: The Invisible Embrace*. "Yet this glimpse grounds everything about your life and illuminates your work, friendships, destiny, and identity." Most importantly, it increases our capacity to love and experience the divine.

Many of us think we know ourselves, but in most cases we're only fooling ourselves. There are at least three reasons why. First, our attention is focused on external circumstances rather than on ourselves. We naturally focus on the external rather than the internal, perhaps because it seems easier to understand our outer world than the inner one. Second, we deceive ourselves. Self-deceit shows up in our lives as denial and blame. These are defense mechanisms we use to combat the fear that if we found out who we really are, we might not like what we find. It's much safer to send what we do not want to face to the shadow. Finally, rarely do we take time for introspection. In our technology-driven, go-go times, we don't value this important practice. We're absorbed with the outside world, and we've neglected spending time within. In the process we have become strangers to our souls.

When we fail to explore our intentions and motivations, our actions are controlled by the unconscious. This means we're basically asleep—living our lives on autopilot. I read once that as many as 90 percent of people live 90 percent of their lives on cruise control. "If we can stay awake when our lives are changing, secrets will be revealed to us—secrets about ourselves, about the nature of life, and about the eternal source of happiness and peace that is always available, always renewable, already within us," writes Elizabeth Lesser in *Broken Open: How Difficult Times Can Help Us Grow*.

Ninety percent of change comes from awareness; the remaining 10 percent is cleanup. So the call to us on the path from the unconscious to the conscious self is to pay attention. Pay attention to our thoughts, feelings, physical sensations, dreams, fantasies, and life events. Everything warrants our attention because everything has the potential to teach us something about our self, our life, and the divine.

John Calvin underscored the absolute necessity of accurate self-knowledge and of knowing God in the opening pages of his monumental work, *Institutes of the Christian Religion*. In it he writes: "Nearly all wisdom we possess, that is to say, true and sound wisdom, consists in two parts: the knowledge of God and of ourselves." Calvin continues: "It is not possible to know God without knowing yourself. It is not possible to know yourself without knowing God." The two are mutually dependent upon one another.

In the next chapter, you'll meet your guide on Path One: your observer or witness self. I encourage you to pay particular attention to this chapter, because it addresses one of the most important topics we will cover. The more you know and call on your observer self, the faster you'll travel all three paths.

CHAPTER FOURTEEN

The Guide: Your Observer Self

There's nothing more critical to your spiritual growth than realizing that you are not the voice in your mind; you are the one who hears it. That's so important that I'm going to repeat it: nothing is more critical to your spiritual growth than realizing you're not the voice in your mind; you're the one who hears it.

Let's do a little experiment. Take a minute and tune into your thoughts. Yes, right now. Put this book aside and tune into your thoughts for a few minutes. Write down each thought as it comes up. Write them all down, no matter how crazy they may be. I just did it, and here's what I wrote:

Oh, they'll never put the book down and do this. They'll continue reading.

I've got just another thirty minutes before I have to be at my meeting.

Gosh, it's a pretty day.

Where is Loodle (my dog)?

Gosh, it's a pretty day.

Where is Loodle (my dog)?

You get the idea. As you can see, my thoughts are mostly inconsequential. It's pretty clear I am not my thoughts. It's like looking into a mirror. I'm not the image—I am the one observing the image. I'm also not my body, and I'm not my personality. I'm even not so much a human being as the consciousness watching that human being.

Can you think of a book that changed your life? I have several, but one of the most important is *The Short Path to Enlightenment: Instructions for Immediate Awakening* by Paul Brunton. Brunton was a British theosophist and spiritualist at the turn of the century and one of the first to popularize Neo-Hindu spiritualism in Western culture. He calls the observing self, "The unchanging consciousness which gives consciousness to the individual." When the observer self is awake, our consciousness is conscious of being conscious. I like to think about the observer self as an uninvolved witness.

Think about it. If the observing self didn't exist, then we would cease to exist because without consciousness—or awareness of our being—we are not here. It kind of blows the mind, doesn't it? The observer self is our first clue that we are more than a series of selves, and learning to identify with the observer self instead of the many disparate selves allows us to experience a more unified self.

Your observer self is your guide on Path One. It helps us connect with our essence, unify our scattered selves, and embark on the spiritual journey of coming home. I remember when I first became aware of my observer self. I was about twelve years old, doing homework, when I had this out-of-body experience. I felt I was both the subject and the observer. I was sitting at my desk while observing myself seated at my desk. I was totally present. It didn't feel scary at the time; it just felt real—like a thin curtain had been pulled back and I was experiencing the world as it really was for the first time.

Four Truths About the Observer Self

Stephen Cope's wonderful book *Yoga and Quest for The True Self* helped me remember four essential truths about the observer self:

Truth One: The witness is always with us. We just need to bring awareness to him or her, and that can be as easy as simply pausing, taking a deep breath, and tuning in.

It's easy to get distracted and forget to tune into the observer self, or to witness. It's then we fall into autopilot and slip into an old, one-dimensional, unconscious way of seeing the world.

Truth Two: When my observer self is at work, it's a whole body experience rather than just an intellectual exercise. For example, I often get nervous walking into a room of strangers, whether it's a cocktail party or an after-hours network event. This often surprises those who know me, but I'm far more comfortable having a one-to-one, in-depth conversation than making small talk in a crowd. When my observer self is on the job, I can observe my discomfort both mentally and physically. I might be entertaining a false belief like "I'm not enough" or "I don't belong" while my throat dries, my palms get damp, and I tense my neck and shoulders.

Truth Three: The observer self does not judge; he or she practices "choiceless awareness." We don't need to choose what to experience—experience happens. We simply have to be with it. When we are judging our experience, we are fighting against it and cannot see that experience for what it is. When judgment does creep in—as it often does—we know that our inner critic has taken over the wheel. Both observe, but only the inner critic judges. To return the wheel to our observer self, we begin observing our judging—without judgment.

Truth Four: The observer self always works in the present. Even if it's dealing with something in our past or future, it's actually observing what is happening *in this moment* as we deal with the past or future.

Hopefully you now have a better understanding of the observer self. If not, I've included a wonderful exercise at the end of this section that will help you experience it firsthand. Now we'll take a look at the chief obstacle and the gift on the evolution from the unconscious to the conscious self.

CHAPTER FIFTEEN

Chief Obstacle and the Gift

You'd think we'd embrace the concept of making what is unconscious conscious—and we do. But as we learned earlier, there's also a part of us that doesn't. Deep down, there's a force within that wants to keep us in the dark. It wants to ignore the truth about ourselves, protect the illusion of innocence, and above all alleviate the fear of having to take responsibility for our lives.

The chief obstacle on the path from the unconscious to the conscious self is irresponsibility, or the avoidance of taking responsibility for our lives. While we may be loath to admit it, there's a part of us that loves being a victim. When we are victims, someone or something else is always to blame. Author Erica Jong once quipped: "Take your life in your own hands, and what happens? A terrible thing: no one to blame."

I love being a victim; it's one of the few times that I allow myself to relax. I'm a bit of a control freak. I feel that if it's going to be done right, then I have to do it. As a result, I'm always hyper-vigilant. When I'm a victim, I'm not to blame, so I can relax my hyper-vigilance. As appealing as this may be, there's a bigger part of me that would rather take responsibility, because with responsibility I'm in more control and can make conscious choices on how to live my life.

The Gift: Choice

When we bring what is unconscious into consciousness, we are given the gift of choice. We can choose how to respond to a situation. When we operate from the unconscious self, we have no choice but to react. We're like puppets being manipulated by the invisible strings of the unconscious. But when we shift from the unconscious to the conscious self, we gain invaluable knowledge about ourselves that allows us to snip those strings, cease automatically reacting to situations, and consciously choose our reactions. Carl Jung sums this truth up nicely: "Until you make the unconscious conscious, it will direct your life and you will call it fate." Jungian scholar and author James Hollis concurs but warns, "What is not conscious owns you, and very little is conscious, even with earnest effort."

Have you ever been around someone who was constantly trying to impress? It can be pretty annoying, can't it? You share a story about your wonderful beach vacation in Florida, and he pipes in about his Caribbean cruise. I used to be that person. It's not that I was a braggart—it's that I wanted you to like me, and I felt I had to impress in order to be worthy of being likeable. Now that I know that about myself, I have a choice. I can try to impress you with a story about wealth, success, adventures, etc., or I can choose to be quiet and listen to you. As I grow spiritually, I'm increasingly opting to be quiet and listen, and in the process I'm finding that I'm creating stronger connections when I do.

We've reviewed quite a lot about Path One. We discussed that the unconscious consists of thoughts, feelings, drives, fantasies, motives, and reactions of which we are unaware, but which influence every aspect of our lives, including mental, emotional, interpersonal, sexual, and professional. We also discussed the interesting relationship between shadow and persona, and how the chief task on Path One—the evolution from unconscious to conscious self—is to know one's self. Many of us think we know ourselves, but we are only fooling ourselves. There's nothing more critical to your spiritual growth than realizing you're not the voice in your mind; you're the one who hears it. This is your observer—or witness—self, and he or she is your guide on Path One.

The chief obstacle on this path is irresponsibility—or avoiding responsibility for our lives, and the gift is choice. The gift of making what is unconscious conscious is that we are able to choose our actions rather than simply react. There are numerous tools that can help bring what is unconscious in our lives to consciousness. Some of my favorites include therapy, journaling, dream work, and art. Hopefully you'll experiment with several to find those that work for you.

In the next chapter I'll share one exercise, one tool, and one practice that I've found particularly helpful on this path. They are an exercise to help better understand the observer self, a psychological-spiritual model called the Enneagram, and a tool to help reclaim projections.

CHAPTER SIXTEEN

Tools, Practices, and Questions

Exercise: Getting to Know Your Observer Self

I detailed this exercise in my book *The Inspired Life: How Connection and Contribution Create Power, Passion, and Joy*. It's actually more of a meditation, and it's adapted from two sources: Roberto Assagioli's disidentification process in psychosynthesis, and Ken Wilber's meditations in *One Taste: Daily Reflection on Integral Spirituality*.

> Close your eyes, take a few deep, centering breaths, and relax your body. Breathe deeply and feel the cool air moving in and out of your nose as you breathe. Tune into your body. Notice how you are sitting, check your posture, and see where you are holding tension.
>
> Say to yourself: "I have a body, but I am not my body."
>
> Take three deep, cleansing breaths. Now focus on your emotions.
>
> What feelings do you notice? Are you restless, anxious, angry, or serene? Observe your current feelings, and then think about the most common feelings in your life. Do not dwell on those feelings—recall and release them.
>
> Say to yourself out loud: "I have feelings, but I am not my feelings."
>
> Take three deep, cleansing breaths.
>
> Move from your feelings to your desires. Desires are those things that motivate us, such as comfort, money, health, or love. Observe the things that motivate you, but do not judge them. Simply call them up and notice them.
>
> Repeat to yourself: "I have desires, but I am not my desires."

Take three deep, cleansing breaths.

Now move to your thoughts. As each thought arises to consciousness, observe it but do not dwell on it. Then watch as the next one rises to replace it, over and over again. Think of your thoughts as clouds. Allow each to float by.

Say silently to yourself or out loud: "I have thoughts, but I am not my thoughts."

Take three deep, cleansing breaths.

Finally, become aware of that part of you that has been observing your body, your feelings, your desires, and your thoughts.

Having detached from the basic elements of consciousness, say to yourself: "I have a body, but I am not my body; I have feelings, but I am not my feelings; I have desires, but I am not my desires; I have thoughts, but I am not my thoughts."

Now ask yourself: what is the source of my awareness?

It's the one who has been watching your sensations, feelings, desires, and thoughts.

This is your observer, or witness, self.

Tool: Shave Years Off Your Therapy with the Enneagram

I'm a huge fan of the Enneagram, which is, among other things, a personality typing system. In fact, I half-jokingly tell clients that the Enneagram can shave "years off your therapy." It has done so for me. The centerpiece of the Enneagram is the structure of nine interrelated strategies for how we relate with ourselves, others, and the world. But what I appreciate most about the Enneagram is that through it, we can identify the chief obstacles that prevent us from living in essence.

Enneagram scholar Stephen Wolinsky has identified nine false core beliefs that underlie each personality type. These false core beliefs reflect early childhood traumas or experiences that, when left unconscious, guide many of our decisions.

Enneagram Type	False Belief
One:	There must be something wrong with me.
Two:	I am worthless.
Three:	I have an inability to …
Four:	I am inadequate.
Five:	I don't exist.
Six:	I am alone.
Seven:	I am incomplete; something is missing.
Eight:	I am powerless.
Nine:	There is no love; this is a loveless world.

Do any of these seem familiar? While we can identify with all nine types, we all have a preference. My preference is Three on the Enneagram. On the surface I appear extremely confident, competent, and convicted. But what most people don't know is that I am filled with self-doubt. Why? Because in many situations, I don't feel capable. Many of my friends are Enneagram Sevens; much of their lives are spent searching for the illusive "missing piece."

All transformation begins with awareness. By identifying the false beliefs that are at play in our lives, we can begin to release them. Identifying false beliefs is only a small part of what the Enneagram has to offer on Path One, Path Two, and Path Three. If you are even slightly intrigued, I highly encourage you to check out the book *The Wisdom of the Enneagram: The Complete Guide to Psychological and Spiritual Growth for the Nine Personality Types* by Don Richard Riso and Russ Hudson.

Practice: Projection, or You Can't See Your Ass Without a Mirror

A friend once told me, "You can't see your ass without a mirror." I laughed, but at the same time saw the wisdom in her quip. Life offers us many mirrors in which to better know ourselves, but I can think of no better one than projection. Projection is a psychological term that has also been called "blame shifting." Instead of taking responsibility for an undesirable impulse or trait, we attribute it to another person.

I have a friend whom I have dinner with periodically who really doesn't get me. I'll be telling a story and he'll chime in with something like, "I bet that made you furious." I'll correct him: "Not really. I thought it was funny." But it's obvious—he's not buying it. Whenever this happens—and it happens a good bit with this friend, I have a strong negative reaction. One solution might be to quit seeing this friend, but I don't want to do that. I love this man. Another option is to take a closer look at my own stuff.

It didn't take long for me to realize that my wounded child was being triggered. As a kid, I felt my parents never got me, because if they did they wouldn't love the real me. When my friend misreads my reactions, these old feelings—and the old limiting belief that I'm not loveable as I am—arise. With this new knowledge, I was then able to take the blame off my friend, find compassion for my woundedness, and soothe that sweet part of me that was crying out for attention. And dinners with my friend improved dramatically.

Another example of projection involves one of my brother's friends, an Episcopal priest, whom I disliked immediately. He struck me as sentimental, overly emotional, and weak. He would tear up at a drop of a hat. Seeing someone so open with emotions struck a raw nerve. Looking closer, I realized I had projected a repressed part of myself onto him. By shining light onto my shadow, I could withdraw my projection and begin the work of reclaiming my emotional side.

Projections can be negative or positive. When I moved to the mountains of North Carolina, I couldn't be around creative people enough. I made friends with artists, writers, poets, and actors. Later, when I reclaimed my own creativity by painting and writing, my attraction lessened. I still enjoy hanging out with my creative friends, but I no longer project my creativity onto them.

Watching out for projection has been one of the most valuable life lessons I've learned, and it's one of the best tools I know to help us know ourselves more fully. I am now on hyper-alert when I have a strong reaction to someone. Whether that reaction is positive or negative, I recognize it as a clue that this person is exhibiting a "shadow" characteristic that I feel I don't have, but actually I do.

Questions

Here are a number of questions to consider. I recommend choosing a few that have some "heat" for you and journaling about them.

1. What wishes to be honored in my life? What areas of my life are being neglected right now?
2. What is waiting to die within me, and what is waiting to give birth?
3. In what areas were my mother and father stuck, and where/how are those issues playing out in my life now?
4. What scares me?
5. Looking back on my life, what causes me guilt? Shame?
6. What is the dominant emotion in my life right now?
7. How would I describe myself? How would others describe me?

In closing, I also find it helpful to explore what's going in my life *at the time it's actually happening*. When a situation happens that gets my attention—whether in a positive or negative way—I like to ask:

1. Could there be something that I'm not seeing about myself or the situation?
2. What could this situation be trying to teach me in this moment?
3. What is making me most uncomfortable about this situation? (Chances are this is where the gold is.)

As you bring more of that which is unconscious into consciousness, you will be invited to examine your defended self. In this process, you will get to know your authentic self. In the next section, we'll explore Path Two.

SECTION V

Path Two: Defended to Authentic Self

Resolution
Nick Lachey

Nothing but an empty page
Breathing in an open space
Captured by your moment's grace again

There's so much I left behind
Even more that waits in time
Everything's so undefined

I'm standing on the edge of my fear
And I see it clear

Here's my resolution
I'm letting go
All I need to learn is along this road
And I just want to be the best man I can be
Breathe, it's my resolution
Living life without a plan
Finding solace where I stand

And learning how to love again

And all I want is something real
That I can feel

Here's my resolution
I'm letting go
All I need to learn is along this road
And I just wanna be the best man I can be

'Cause here's my resolution
I'm letting go
All I need to learn is along this road
And I just wanna be the best man I can be
Breathe, it's my resolution
My resolution

The Beauty of Vulnerability

Recently I sat on my therapist's maroon corduroy sofa and shared several insights that I had discovered the week before concerning my feelings about intimacy. As I talked, my therapist listened while taking detailed notes. When I wrapped up my forty-minute monolog, she asked several probing questions. I answered. Then our eyes met, and she was silent. One minute…perhaps two…passed. I panicked. I felt vulnerable, naked, and exposed. And I felt busted. I had been sharing some of my deepest thoughts and feelings, but I had not been sharing them *with her*. I had become disassociated from my feelings, and my therapist had become no more than a receptacle for my words.

Growing up, I had learned that expressing emotions was too risky. I would become too vulnerable, and if I were too vulnerable I would be crushed. Taunts of "Only sissies cry," and "Be a man," still ring in my ears. Emotions were something that "real men" didn't dare show, and I was always under intense pressure to be "a real man."

There are three centers of intelligence: the head, the heart, and the gut. In an effort to prove my masculinity, I learned to communicate using only one of these centers: the head. While this strategy helped me feel safe, it prevented me from experiencing real connection.

How different my experience would have been that day in my therapist's office if I had communicated from my head, gut, and heart. We could have connected in that silence, and I could have experienced the comfort of feeling seen, heard, understood, and loved for all I am. Today, expressing emotions is still difficult for me, but increasingly I'm finding the courage to express them, and in doing so I'm forging deeper connections in a way I've never experienced before.

In this section, we'll talk about the defended and the authentic selves. We'll discuss defense mechanisms, core wounds, and attributes of the authentic self. I'll explain that the central task of Path Two is to know one's true self, and we'll review seven strategies for accomplishing this task. We will also discuss the guide, the chief obstacle, and the gift of this path, and we'll conclude the section with several tools, practices, and questions that will assist you on your journey.

CHAPTER SEVENTEEN

Meet the Defended Self

We know we are operating from our defended self when we are experiencing:

- Grudges
- Shame
- Specialness
- Scarcity Thinking
- Savior Seeking
- Comparing
- Envy
- Taking people, places, and things for granted
- Inflexibility
- Labeling/Defining
- Having to be right
- Possessiveness
- Pride
- Investing in a role(s)
- Any "isms," such as alcoholism
- Clinging
- Expecting
- Anticipating
- Assuming
- Knowing
- Thinking we have all the answers
- Classifying/Categorizing
- Objectifying
- Rejecting
- Projecting
- Defending
- Interpreting
- Fearing
- Judging
- Avoiding
- Ignoring
- Seeking pleasure
- Avoiding pain
- Planning
- Pleasing
- Seeking stability

That's quite a list. If you're like me, you recognize a good many of these. We all do. That's because—whether we are conscious of it or not—we operate from the defended self a good bit in our lives. Most of the behaviors on this list are defense mechanisms that we employ to protect us from childhood wounds. We all have them. We can have the greatest parents in the world who love us unconditionally, and still we will have wounds. Few—if any—parents can meet all their child's needs while positively reinforcing their essence.

In order to know the defended self, we must become conscious of this childhood wounding. Jungian analyst, author, and friend Bud Harris counsels, "Becoming conscious of the effects of the wounds and traumas of our childhood and the influence of the social character on our development is the first step toward attaining individual consciousness." When Harris suggests that we become aware of the "the effects" of the wounds of our childhood, he's referring to the pain they caused us.

Know Your Life Themes

Some call them core wounds. In her books, *When You Think You're Not Enough: The Four Life-Changing Steps To Loving Yourself* and *The Ten Things to Do When Your Life Falls Apart: An Emotional and Spiritual Handbook*, Daphne Rose Kingma has a different take. Instead of core wounds she offers six life themes, defined as significant psychological issues that are created in childhood and reinforced when similar events with the same emotional charge reoccur throughout our lives. Kingma's six life themes are:

1. Neglect
2. Abandonment
3. Abuse
4. Rejection
5. Emotional Suffocation
6. Deprivation

Looking over Kingma's life themes, which look familiar? If you are like me you can identify with several. My dad was a workaholic (abandonment) and my mother treated me as a spouse (emotional suffocation). While these two themes affect my life, rejection is probably the strongest of Kingma's life themes for me.

My mother was thirty-nine when she became pregnant with me. My brothers were eleven and twelve when I was born. To say I was a surprise is putting it nicely. My mother did not want to be pregnant. I internalized her anxiety in the womb and entered this world justifying my existence by seeking approval from Mom, Dad, and from just about anyone else. Seeking approval is my defense mechanism of choice for my issues around fear of abandonment. And if I allow it, it can become a motivating factor for almost every decision in my life.

Delving deeper, I now understand that power and powerlessness are also emotional consequences of the themes at play in my life. As a child, my bedroom closet was my secret sanctuary. There I retreated into the fantasy world of my imagination, my only defense against the powerlessness I felt as a child. Dressing up in flowing red robes, crowns, and crosses, I became a man of authority, power, and control. In my closet I was king to my parents' pawn. I was lord over my destiny. Yet, I would have gladly traded my crown for the ability to live in a world where my authentic personhood could thrive.

The more I think about it, power, powerlessness, control, and surrender are universal principles that impact all our lives. We all want to feel more in control, when in truth we have no control over the external part of our lives. The ego is all about control, and control is all about fear. Control helps us protect ourselves from pain, and protecting ourselves from pain is the central role of the defended self.

This strategy may work for a while, but as Michael A. Singer explains in his powerful book *The Untethered Soul*, "You will get to a point in your growth where you understand that if you protect yourself, you will never be free." And you will never grow. Life may feel safer, but it will become stagnant. If we are to grow and experience the freedom of becoming our authentic self, we must leave behind the safety of the defended self.

CHAPTER EIGHTEEN

Meet the Authentic Self

Dr. Phil McGraw may well be the most recognized mental health professional in the world. As the host of a popular talk show and author of numerous books and magazine articles, "Dr. Phil" has worked tirelessly to make psychology accessible to the general public. Dr. Phil defines the authentic self as, "the you that can be found at your absolute core. It is the part of you that is not defined by your job, your function or role." He distinguishes between "authentic" and "fictional" selves, describing the fictional self as: "When you're not living faithfully to your authentic self, you find yourself feeling incomplete, as if there is a hole in your soul."

I knew I was gay as long as I can remember; yet I chose to live a straight life. Some may judge me. To them I say, walk a mile in my shoes. For me, being gay was simply not an option. Everything that mattered to me hinged on being a mainstream married man. To earn my parents' approval, I sought to be successful. I wanted to prove to them I could succeed. By being known in business, community, and society, I thought I could earn their love and respect.

Standard issue for success was a spouse, so I married. I honestly believed I could make it work. I loved my wife and thought I could overcome my homosexuality. On our honeymoon night, I awoke with a jolt realizing what I had done. I was using my wife to shield my sexuality. I sold my soul to achieve success. In order to fit in, I denied myself my true emotions, my true self, and my emotional core. Regardless, I saw no other option. Heterosexuality was the price of admission. Only by appearing straight could I be admitted into the good old boys club.

In the 1970s being gay wasn't for sissies. Gay men and women had to be tough. Society wasn't nearly as accepting as it is now. Back then, executives married, few divorced, and none that I knew were gay. The gay men I did know of were waiters, hairdressers, and retail clerks. I knew not one gay person who met my definition of success.

As a straight man, my career flourished. My wife and I achieved a place in society, and I was accepted in an old-line private club in Atlanta.

Appearing straight helped me achieve the trappings of success and live the American Dream. While I may have fulfilled my parents' expectations, I still felt empty. Their definition of success didn't bring me the happiness they promised. The American Dream turned into my nightmare, and the trappings of success became my jail. By focusing on my parents' desires, I neglected my needs. I ransomed my authenticity for approval, and it was much too high a price to pay.

I was lonely. I felt isolated. The secret of my sexuality had barred love and intimacy from my life. Craving connection, I cried out, "Enough!" At age thirty-nine, I found the courage to claim my authentic self. My parents were both dead, and my oldest brother had come out years before me. Even so, I expected to lose everything that defined me, including all the people I loved. At midlife I was giving up far more than I would have at sixteen. But none of that mattered. I had to come out or die.

I was surprised when I didn't have to give up titles, salary, or social standing. By that point, attitudes toward homosexuality had evolved. Today most gay men and women can achieve success and still be their true selves. I pray that this greater acceptance will continue and that gay men and women come out earlier than I did, and in the process avoid hurting those they love most.

My heart still hurts when I remember the sadness, disillusionment, and betrayal my ex-wife must have felt throughout the period of my coming out and our subsequent divorce. She didn't deserve such pain—no one does.

My coming-out experience shaped me into who I am today. I have experienced both heterosexual and homosexual worlds, and today I live in a world of my own creation—a world in which my personhood can thrive. Coming out entails self-examination, self-discovery, and self-acceptance. Only at midlife did I face old fears, find my true self, and start anew. I found coming out was far more than claiming sexuality; for me, coming out was about reclaiming my authentic self.

I read once that the most important thing is to be who you are without shame. When we are newborn babies, we know who we are. We know our wants, needs, and feelings, and we express them freely. We are our authentic selves. But as we get older, we are taught that in order to fit in and be loved, we must give up select aspects of ourselves—including certain needs, wants, and feelings. No one escapes from socialization entirely, but if any of us ever hope to live a rich, joy-filled, and meaningful life, we must seek to reclaim that authentic self.

When we reclaim our authentic selves, we begin to:
- Give ourselves permission to be all we are;
- Realize that we are enough—just the way we are;
- Refuse to allow others' expectations, opinions, moods, or emotions dominate us;
- Express a full range of emotions, including those we deem negative;
- Speak our truth. When we have a conflict with someone, we talk to him or her about it directly. We also don't back down when someone challenges or disagrees with us;
- Ask for help or support when we need it;
- Say "no" when we don't want to do something;
- Admit when we are wrong and apologize if necessary;
- Know what matters to us in life and prioritize our lives accordingly;
- Find our passion and use it and our unique skills and talents to benefit others.

As you can see from this list, the authentic self is not only who we are, but also what we become; it's not so much an event as it is a process. And it's a process that never ceases. "To be nobody but myself in a world which is doing its best night and day to make me someone else means to fight the hardest battle any human can fight, and never stop fighting," wrote e.e. cummings.

CHAPTER NINETEEN

The Evolution from the Defended to the Authentic Self

"'Know Thyself' was written over the portal of the antique world," wrote Irish writer Oscar Wilde. "Over the portal of the new world, '*Be Thyself*' shall be written." Path One's central task is to know one's self, while Path Two calls us to become our true self. American spiritual teacher, philosopher, and author Vernon Howard writes, "The genuinely spiritual person is one who has lost all desire to be anyone but exactly who he is, without labels and without apologies. He is what he is and that's all there's to it. Such a man is undivided, uncomplicated, and contented."

After coming out to my wife of fourteen years, I moved out. Opening the door to my new apartment, I faced an uncertain future with fear. I had moved from a 3,500 square-foot home to an apartment so small that friends would dub it the "penalty box." The apartment was indeed modest size, and it felt like a sanctuary to me. This safe space would become a place for introspection, healing, and growth. The smell of fresh paint and newly-laid carpet signaled a new beginning. The persona that I had so perfectly constructed for many years had cracked, and in time would crumble and dissolve into dust.

That night as I lay in bed, I stared into the darkness and tossed and turned. Eyes wide open, I clutched my pillow and waited for the morning. "There will be light," my older brother advised. "But you'll have to walk through the darkness to get to it." Coming out was the hardest thing I've ever done—and the most profound. Once I surrendered my secret, it lost its power over me and I could begin living an authentic life. I could walk in the light.

"To thine own self be true," spoke Polonius wisely in Shakespeare's *Hamlet*. While there are many strategies we could employ to follow this sage advice, seven have been particularly helpful to me, and I'd like to share them with you. They are:

1. Make peace with pain;
2. Befriend your shadow;
3. Put your persona in perspective;
4. Burst the bubble of your reality;
5. Know what truly matters to you;
6. Express yourself;
7. Follow your internal GPS system.

Let's explore each of these in more detail.

CHAPTER TWENTY

Make Peace with Pain

My dear friend Ruth is a gifted teacher. One of her favorite sayings is, "In order to know *who* you are, you must know *where* you are." Ruth teaches that being our authentic self starts with fully experiencing each moment; for only when we fully see, taste, hear, smell, and feel them can we learn what we are and be who we are. This requires us to be with *all* our experiences—even emotions that we consider painful.

Make peace with pain? You've got to be kidding! Who wants to make peace with pain?

Well I do, and so do you. Freedom is worth it.

Almost thirty years have passed since my mother died. She was the taproot of our family tree. During her last few years, visiting her hospital room was a daily ritual for my two brothers and me. Through these visits, doctor conferences, and the process of updating family friends, my brothers and I grew closer. Looking back, I believe this was Mother's plan. She knew she was our touchstone, and she worried we would drift apart after she died. Our lives were so different, and in many ways she was our only connection.

Her death was a slow one. It often is with cancer. After she died, our family seemed to fall apart; two coming-outs and three divorces followed. Yet the brothers stayed together. Despite my love for my mother, I could not grieve her death. The pain of losing her was too intense. My feelings froze the day she died.

At her service, a flood of emotions raged deep below the surface, yet I couldn't cry. I feared I might lose control. If I wasn't careful I feared I would sink so deep that I could never resurface. Family friends with casseroles, flowers at the funeral, and the long limousine ride home followed. Looking back, it's all little more than blurry memories… a surreal dream faded over time.

After the service I barricaded myself in her kitchen, feeling unable to face the host of friends who came to pay their respects. I was afraid to see my own pain mirrored in their eyes. So instead of facing this pain, I shut off my emotions and lost my emotional core. Blocking emotions in one area of my life meant blocking them all. If loving someone meant losing that person, I could not risk loving. I pledged I would never again feel like an abandoned child.

For ten years I was disconnected with people—even those I loved most. I was numb. Then an incident triggered a memory of her death and the ice began melting. My lover at the time was facing challenges as he started a new career, and I watched as his mother provided loving support to him. Seeing this mother-son connection jolted my emotions from their sleep. His mother's intense concern, sincere sympathy, and love made me long for my own mother. Never had I felt so alone. I felt raw, vulnerable, and lonely. I spent more time by myself, and shed tears while watching even the most benign television shows. I flinched at seemingly innocent comments. I missed my mother so much my stomach ached.

But instead of masking the pain, I leaned into it. I turned the wheel into the skid. I felt the truth, followed its thread, and found that a large chunk of my heart had gone missing. "I came to explore the wreck," poet Adrienne Rich wrote. "I came to see the damage that was done and the treasure that prevailed."

Exploring the Wreck

A while back, I kept drawing the same tarot card as a part of my daily meditation. The card read: Aloneness, Not Loneliness. I had been single for a long stretch, and the weekends were still tough. Try as I might, I felt lonely. It seemed the rest of the world was enjoying leisure time with loved ones while I struggled to fill the hours. I hate self-pity, and I abhor playing the role of the victim. At the same time I have to admit it felt good feeling sorry for myself.

Well-meaning friends counseled me to stay active: join special interest groups, volunteer, and call folks to go to the movies. Their advice was sound—activity had always helped numb the pain in the past. But something was different this time; I had this knowing that it was time to sit with my sadness. I had to be with it, rather than understand it or make it go away. The following weekend I resolved not to judge my feelings, but to give myself permission to feel them. If I felt sad, I would feel sad. I told myself there was nothing to be afraid of. What I found was that emotions only last a few seconds, but I continued to play them in my mind—refusing to let them go.

In his book *The Power of the Supermind,* Vernon Howard calls this process "mental movies." Mental movies make us miserable, and they abuse the imagination. We have a painful experience with someone, then run it over and over in our minds visualizing what he said, what we did, how we both felt. We run the clip day and night. "It is as if you were locked inside a theater playing a horrible movie," Howard observes.

Much later, a wise therapist taught me a new way for dealing with these unpleasant emotions. Our conversation went something like this:

"Recently I've lost my center, and I feel a bit out of control," I said. "I feel as if I am on a train, the conductor has left his post, and we are traveling at warp speed."

"So take a deep breath," she said, and I did.

"Now who is in the conductor's seat?"

"I am."

"Why do you think that is?" she asked.

"I am aware of what's going on," I replied.

"So you are conscious of your consciousness?"

"Yes. My Observer Self."

"So you know how to flick off the auto pilot, right? Simply tune into your Observer Self."

"I agree."

"Then why aren't you doing it?" she probed.

"I'm not sure."

"Guess."

I was avoiding something, and she knew it. She knows me too well. Instead of being with such difficult emotions as sadness and anger, I tend to numb out or fast forward through them.

"I want you to see the pain as energy. There's nothing to be afraid of. Just allow it to pass through you by identifying with the part of you that is watching all of this," she directed.

My therapist then helped me objectify the pain by imagining it as a physical object. Eckhart Tolle calls this the "pain body."

"Where is it now in your body?" she asked.

"Right in my chest," I replied.

"How big is it?" she probed.

"About the size of a grapefruit."

"And its consistency?" she continued.

"Again, a grapefruit."

"Take a deep breath," she said.

I did.

"Now where is it?"

"It's shifted," I notice. "It's closer to my throat."

"And the size?"

"It's a bit smaller. The size of a baseball."

"Consistency?" she asked.

"Harder. Like an apple."

We continued like this for a while. The pain continued to shift and diminish until eventually it passed.

It's hard to imagine what it would be like to be at peace with pain, but when we are not we devote our life to avoiding it. Again, pain is energy, and as such we want it to pass through us rather than get stuck. By objectifying and tracking it *as it occurs*, we learn that pain is always changing—and when we attend to it, it will eventually pass through us.

I am learning that one of the biggest obstacles to my ability to love is the belief that I must protect myself from difficult emotions such as sadness and feeling unworthy. I am also learning that the only way to face them is head on—by finding the courage to be present with them when they arise.

CHAPTER TWENTY-ONE

Befriend Your Shadow

We've already talked a bit about shadow in our discussion of the unconscious self. Again, the shadow represents all the parts of ourselves that we don't acknowledge. In order to reclaim our authentic selves, we must recognize and accept even those parts of ourselves that bring pain, discomfort, and shame. While one task on Path One is to identify our shadow, our task on Path Two is a bit harder: it's to accept and integrate it. "Seeing your lower self is one thing," a client bemoaned. "Learning to accept—much less appreciate—it is another." She's right. Learning to accept, appreciate, even love those aspects of ourselves that we find less desirable is one of the hardest tasks we're asked to do in life, yet it is crucial if we're to become the full expression of all we are. When we can accept ourselves without judgment, we can accept others—and this is when true connection takes place.

In accepting and ultimately loving those aspects of self that we've deemed negative, it's helpful to remember that God made us the way we are. As such we are expressions of the divine. We are an intentional design, and I believe that we are brought into this world with a lower and higher nature to teach us specific lessons. There's a beautiful story about the prodigal son from the Bible that illustrates this point. Perhaps you remember it—it goes something like this:

A man had two sons. The younger son told his father, "I want my share of your estate now, instead of waiting until you die." So his father agreed to divide his wealth between his two sons.

A few days later this younger son packed all his belongings and took a trip to a distant land. While there he wasted all his money on wild living. About the time his money ran out, a great famine swept over the land, and he began to starve. He persuaded a local farmer to hire him to feed his pigs. The boy became so hungry that even the pods he fed the pigs looked better than what he was eating.

When he finally came to his senses, he said to himself, "At home, even the hired men have food enough to spare, and here I am dying of hunger! I will go home to my father and say, "Father, I have sinned against both heaven and you, and I am no longer worthy of being called your son. Please take me on as a hired hand."

So he returned home to his father. And while he was still a long distance away, his father saw him coming. Filled with love and compassion, he ran to his son, embraced and kissed him. His son said to him, "Father, I have sinned against both heaven and you, and I am not worthy to be called your son."

But his father said to the servants, "Quick! Bring the finest robe in the house and put it on him. Get a ring for his finger and sandals for his feet. And kill the calf we have fattened in the pen. We must celebrate with a feast, for this son of mine was dead and now has returned to life. He was lost, but now he is found."

Like most parables, this one has several interpretations. For the purposes of our discussion, we'll explore this one: only when the ego (son) assimilates his shadow, as symbolized by feeding the swine, can it be reunited with essence (his father).

"We build our shadow as we build our identity (persona). They're like two sides of the same coin. Every time we identify with a value growing up…, we reject its opposite…." writes Jungian psychiatrist Bud Harris, author of *Sacred Selfishness*. Not only do we need to befriend our shadows, we also want to ensure that we don't put too much emphasis on building and maintaining our persona.

CHAPTER TWENTY-TWO

Put Your Persona in Perspective

Swiss psychiatrist Carl Jung described the persona as a compromise between our society's expectations and our true self. Personas are essential if we're going to live successfully in this world. We use them to make specific impressions in order to facilitate communication and to protect our inner life. However, personas can become dangerous when we become over-identified with them. When this happens, we may:

- Become dependent on others' expectations of us to the point that we don't take risks;
- Believe what we do is who we are;
- Block people from seeing who we really are. Like a turtle that draws up in its shell, we are so defensive that we don't allow others to see our face;
- Forget who we really are. We may have trouble distinguishing between our persona and personhood. It's important to keep both in perspective.

If we are to lead a conscious life, it's imperative to align who we are (authentic self) with who we have come to believe ourselves to be (our persona). When I ended my career in public relations and moved to Asheville, I planned to take six months off. Stripped of titles, roles, and a full calendar, I felt like the emperor with no clothes. I was exposed, uncomfortable, and uncertain. To soothe my discomfort, I immediately launched into a new venture—I started my column, *Confessions of a Late Bloomer*. Soon it was a success. Alternative newspapers across the country began to carry it, and I garnered a loyal following. But this success did not soothe me as it once had. I was still unsure of who I was and what I wanted. In order to find the serenity I sought, I would have to do some "self work" to separate persona from my personhood.

Asheville turned out to be a good place for this. Unlike Atlanta, few people knew me and I could start anew. Slowly I began to learn that people could like me for me—not just for my success. In fact, I learned most people weren't that interested in what I did for a living; they wanted to know how I lived my life. I came to see that keeping personas in perspective is vital to keeping them healthy.

I now know the importance of ensuring that my persona reflects my true nature. Equally important, I've come to realize that I am not my persona; it is only a small dimension of who I am.

CHAPTER TWENTY-THREE

Burst the Bubble

I first heard of the term "bubble" from my friend and spiritual guide Shirley Stinard. Shirley defines the bubble as our virtual reality, or the mini-universes we create from select aspects of ourselves rather than the entirety of our personhood. The bubble is based on the story we create to explain how and why we operate in the world the way we do.

In his book *The Mandala of Being: Discovering the Power of Awareness,* Dr. Richard Moss explains that we create our worldview in our first few years based upon how our parents and other caregivers respond and relate to us, as well as how they care for themselves and each other. And that worldview never changes until we change our selves. The characters may change—we can substitute partners for mom or dad, and even friends may take the place of a sibling, parent, or other significant person in our early life. But the story line often remains the same. I have at times helped clients change jobs only to have them wind up in the same situation they just left. I've done the same in romantic relationships. The thing we have to remember is the consistent variable in these unhappy work situations and romantic relationships is us.

Moss writes, "When we live in a recurrent constellation of me stories, we are likely to feel sad because we are unconsciously defending an identity that does not represent our true fullness." It helps to remember that we change from moment to moment, and the only way to truly know oneself is to be present to oneself in that moment. So when that old story pops up, instead of stopping, fighting, or fabricating a more desirable one, simply say "this is an old story." By doing so we become present, stop resisting our experience, and eventually see how the mind is distorting reality.

I admit that this is much easier said than done. I still find that I'm not always aware that I'm in an old story. The good news is that I'm catching myself more and more. A while ago I was visiting Canyon Ranch Spa in Tucson, Arizona for a workshop on body image. There were six of us, all seated around a rectangular mahogany conference table. A behavioral therapist leading the group said, "Let's begin by introducing ourselves. State your name, where you are from, and your relationship with your body." We were total strangers, yet one by one we opened up and shared our stories. It was my turn.

"I was a fat kid," I started. "No matter how fit I become, I still feel like that fat kid wearing Husky™ pants." The group empathized. An attractive heavyset woman in riding shorts was next. "I came to your group last year and it changed my life," she told the therapist. "I realized the goal was not so much to lose fat as to be fit. No matter how thin I get, I will never look like the models in those magazines, but I can be healthy. It's when I began to see myself as an athlete that my body image changed. I am now thirty pounds thinner, and I have never felt better in my life. Thank you!" Her story sparked an epiphany.

Always the last to be chosen for the team in junior high school, I was overweight, uncoordinated, and had no interest in team sports. I was the antithesis of an athlete. But now at midlife, the story has changed. I am fit. In fact, I've never been in better shape. And I now love walking, biking, and lifting weights. The script changed, but I was still playing the same role.

The following morning I met a group of bikers for a fourteen-mile trek through the desert. The group leader discouraged a mother and daughter from going, stating it was one of the ranch's most strenuous rides. Looking around at the remaining riders in their biking pants, gloves, and cleated shoes, I began to have doubts. "What if I can't keep up?" I fretted. Then standing a little taller, I remembered that I am an athlete. Not only did I complete the ride, but I also finished before most of my fellow riders. The bubble was burst. The fat little boy who was the last to be picked for teams is now a part of my past. In his place, I see an athlete.

I once read a guest column written by Terri Schanks for Krista Tippett's blog, *On Being*. In it, Schanks shares what it means to burst the bubble:

> *And I can only aspire to let go of the stories that no longer serve me or the highest and best good, mindfully and with compassion. I can aspire to release the judgments about good and bad, right or wrong, life or death, all of the dualities held in what I label my experience. And in doing so, I trust all the stories containing my life force somehow blend into a cohesive whole, somehow benefit all beings, are somehow swept into the wispy places where memories go, trusting that like a child blowing bubbles, they are carried away on the breath of giggles.*

CHAPTER TWENTY-FOUR

Know What Truly Matters

When I work with clients, I often help them develop external and internal purpose statements. An external purpose statement identifies how the client wants to be of service to the world; the internal one details how the client wants to live his or her life. One of the easiest ways to develop an internal purpose statement is to identify one's core values, such as integrity, beauty, and connectedness. Core values form our internal navigation systems or codes for living. They represent our personal theology, and they point the way home to our authentic and highest self.

While our core values will most likely remain consistent in our lives for longer lengths of time, we may place more emphasis on one over the others during different periods in our lives. In the first stage of life, we may seek to discover our place in the world. According to author and lecturer James Hollis, the primary question for the first half of life becomes "What is the world asking of me?" During this stage we respond to parental and societal expectations, including identifying a vocation, building a career, finding a life partner, and for many, having children.

Hollis reminds us that around our late thirties and forties (although it can happen at any time) our focus shifts from a biological and social agenda (the outer world) to one concerned with psychological and spiritual issues (our inner world). But if in the second half of life, we continue to focus on matters concerning our financial and emotional security and gaining the approval of others, we diminish our lives—or as Jung wrote, we "walk in shoes too small."

As I wrote earlier, I was thirty-nine when I became dissatisfied with my life and began shifting values. At that time I asked myself some tough questions, and I've included them at the end of this section. These questions helped me uncover my core values and find what I needed for a life that truly satisfied my soul. Today I'm still asking these questions. The answers come slowly, but they do come—allowing me to live more authentically and lead a more meaningful life. And the key to living more authentically and leading a more meaningful life is identifying our core values.

If you want to know what your true core values are, you only have to look as far as the life you are currently living. Everything in your life must have value, or it wouldn't be there. Take a close look at the roles you are currently playing. Prominent roles in mine include mentor, partner, teacher, and artist, so my list of current core values includes teaching, love, and creativity. At the end of this section, I've included another exercise that will help you identify your core values. But for now, let's move onto strategy six.

CHAPTER TWENTY-FIVE

Express Yourself

When I was ten, my parents built their dream house: a one story, white columned Colonial, sited in a brand new subdivision in northwest Atlanta. My room was painted an awful shade of baby blue, had generic framed prints on the walls, and sported blue Armstrong™ linoleum on the floor. I hated it. My parents couldn't have selected a room that reflected my personality less. Within months I moved into my brother's room and made it my own. My brother was off at college and seldom returned home. While mother did not allow me to change the paint colors, furniture, fabrics, or how things were arranged, I was allowed to hang several of my rock posters and a knock-off cardboard Calder mobile.

I think about that awful baby blue room often because it is a metaphor for my early days. With their best intentions, my parents prepared me for a life that they felt would make me safe and successful, but like that room they didn't take into account my passions, interests, and values.

Today, my home is a reflection of my most authentic self—as is my life. There are many ways that we express our authentic selves to the world. We'll explore three: expressing a full range of emotions; creativity; and naming, claiming, and using our strengths.

As we discussed earlier, most of us would rather eat glass than deal with pain. An authentic life is one that expresses a full range of emotions, including those that we may consider unpleasant. Authenticity feeds on creativity, and creativity feeds on authenticity. As an artist, I've seen that when I sacrifice my self, my voice, and/or my vision in order to be accepted, generate sales, get press, or garner approval, I block creativity from flourishing.

Our souls crave to express themselves creatively. "Wait just a minute, Randy," you might be thinking, "I'm not creative." While it may be true that you're not an artist, the chances are quite good that you're creative, and in some way or another you're expressing yourself creatively. It may be in the way you parent, cook, garden, fix things, solve problems, or even manage your money. All of us are creative, and when we act on that creativity we find something more valuable than what we produce for the outside world.

We are at our creative best when we express what is most authentic and unique about us. Creative expression helps us learn about hidden aspects of ourselves, express that which cannot be put in words, and sometimes it helps us express feelings that are too painful to bear at the time. After the break-up with the first man I lived with after my marriage, I was devastated and started attending several ecstatic dance groups in Asheville—some of which are based on the *5Rhythms* work of Gabrielle Roth. Dancing as much as three times a week helped me dance through my pain. Today I paint, shoot photography, and write, and through these forms of creative expression I'm able to speak my truth and express emotions—such as sadness, anger, and frustration—that I had difficulty expressing before.

Finally, a third way that we can express our authenticity is by identifying, claiming, and sharing our gifts with the world. I believe that each of us has a special gift: something we can offer the world in a way that no one else can. I also believe if we are to live a meaningful life we must discover that gift, claim it, and put it to service in the world. The world is full of stories of people whose lives were changed once they discovered their gift and put it out in the world. One of my favorites is that of cooking legend Julia Child, one of the country's first celebrity chefs.

In her early professional life, Child was a copywriter who landed a job with the Office of Strategic Services (OSS), a predecessor of the Central Intelligence Agency (CIA). After the war ended, she and her husband moved to Paris where he introduced her to fine cuisine. She was thirty-six when she enrolled at the famous Le Cordon Bleu cooking school where she studied with other master chefs and went on to spend the rest of her life sharing her love of French cooking with audiences in America as a famous author and television personality.

For some of us it's easy to identify our gifts. We've known them for as long as we can remember. For others it may require some detective work, including asking friends and family, taking personality and skill inventories, exploring our interests and passions and of course, following our internal GPS system.

CHAPTER TWENTY-SIX

Follow Your Internal GPS

Some time ago a friend observed that most of my life's accomplishments were achieved because of a "sheer force of will." At the time I took it as a compliment, but at this point in my life I no longer do. When I'm using sheer force of will to move my life forward, I'm not following my internal GPS system. I'm going against the flow. That's because I'm not operating from my authentic self—I'm operating from fear.

After my divorce I was desperate to fill the void my wife left. I attacked this need like I did everything back then—with sheer force of will. I set up several online profiles, asked friends to set me up, and joined several organizations in an attempt to meet someone. I dated a lot but made no real connections.

After consciously traveling Paths One, Two, and Three, my strategy changed—and it changed without me even realizing it at the time. Instead of pushing my energy outward, I went within. Instead of hunting, I began attracting love into my life. I began by clearing out those obstacles to love, such as blame, projections, and childhood wounds, all while trusting in the divine order and knowing that when the timing was right, love would come.

Going within allowed me to tune into my internal GPS system. Call it inner knowing, higher self, higher power, God, or whatever, but there's a universal wisdom—or internal GPS system—that's available to all of us if only we trust it. One way essence communicates with us is through our internal GPS, and one way our internal GPS communicates with us is through imagination. Think of imagination as "image making"; the soul produces images, symbols, dreams, and fantasies just as the mind produces words, ideas, thoughts, and abstractions.

Okay, but how do we know if we are operating from our internal GPS system or something else? Simple. Stop what you're doing and scan your body for resistance. Ask yourself, "Do I really want to do this?" If you sense resistance or fear, your internal GPS system may be sending a warning that there's division within you and the timing may not be right.

Guidance comes from two sources: intuitive process and intuitive channels. Intuition, or the intuitive process, comes from our higher self, and intuitive channels come from our higher power. When we trust that guidance will come, it comes forth, but the answers may not be what we expect. We have to first trust in our intuition and then interpret its voice. Once again, energy can assist us.

I know I am on the right track when I'm energized, and I know I'm off track when I feel drained. Some years ago my analyst posed the question: "What would your life be like if you were to simply follow your energy?" In this question I found a compass for my calling. Whether it's called energy, enthusiasm, passion, or love, it's all the same to me—when I follow it, I am in the flow. The right situations, people, and resources come forward. I am following what Joseph Campbell called "my bliss." At the same time, when energy and enthusiasm begin to wane, it's time to consider moving on.

For more than fifteen years, I taught two workshops—one on presentation skills and the other on how to package, present, and promote yourself at work. I conducted these workshops twice a year at the University of Georgia's MBA school. These workshops were based, in part, on two books I had written: *PowerHouse Presenting* and *Engineer Your Career*. Working with these men and women was a highlight of my work, but after eight years my energy started to wane. A year later, I made the decision to resign after completing one more set of workshops. Before I could inform the university of my decision, I received a call from my contact there saying how sorry they were, but the funding for my program had been cut. A coincidence? I don't think so. Synchronicity? You bet!

"Synchronicity" is a term coined by Carl Jung for meaningful coincidences. Jung believed that while events may be connected by causality, they also may be connected by meaning. At certain times in our lives, events can line up to guide us in a direction that is in our highest and best good. When we follow our internal GPS system, we can expect synchronicities to show up more frequently in our lives.

Following our internal GPS requires us to follow our energy. As a communications and leadership trainer and coach, organizations would retain me to coach high-potential employees and low-performing staff. A few of the men and women would balk when I first suggested that they follow their energy. "That's maybe all well and good for some," one woman retorted, "but I'm the chief breadwinner in my family. I cannot afford to do what I love." I disagreed.

Her boss had sent her to me because she was failing to live up to her potential. I quickly ascertained that while she was extremely talented, she was in the wrong work environment. She and her boss had totally different working styles, and consequently they clashed. My client had been miserable for years in this position, but was afraid to change jobs for fear she'd never find another job that paid as much. With my encouragement she began to explore the idea of creating her own consultancy. Today she's her own boss and making as much money as she did in her previous job. She found the courage to follow her energy, and now she couldn't be happier.

To review, seven strategies can assist in the evolution from the defended to the authentic self. They are:

1. Make peace with pain;
2. Befriend your shadow;
3. Put your persona in perspective;
4. Burst the bubble;
5. Know what truly matters to you;
6. Express yourself;
7. Follow your internal GPS system.

Now we'll discuss the guide, chief obstacle, and the gift for Path Two.

CHAPTER TWENTY-SEVEN

The Guide, Chief Obstacle, and Gift

The guide for Path Two—the evolution from defended to authentic self—is the courageous self. In order to be our authentic self, we must become vulnerable, and to become vulnerable requires courage—a lot of it. When we allow our underbelly to show, we expose ourselves to the frightening possibilities of being belittled, humiliated, rejected, judged, criticized, and attacked.

Dr. Brené Brown is a research professor at the University of Houston, and her 2010 TEDx Houston talk, *The Power of Vulnerability*, is one of the top five most viewed TED talks in the world. Brown says vulnerability is our most accurate measure of courage. Shedding mom's, dad's, the church's, and society's expectations takes courage, but it's also imperative if you want to become the person you want to be. I remember when my sister-in-law declared she no longer wanted to be the preacher's daughter. No longer did she feel she had to be the perfect example. Another friend left a lucrative job as a lawyer to become an entrepreneur, much to the chagrin of his family and friends. Still another friend left the Mormon Church even though his family threatened to disown him. Look at your own life and the lives of your friends— I'm sure you'll find many more examples of men and women who found the courage to be their authentic selves.

Chief Obstacle: Status Quo

Along Path Two, the chief obstacle—or the ego's strongest defense—is the status quo. Soon after our sweet dog, Loodle the Poodle, came to live with us, we purchased an invisible fence. Loodle wore a special collar that emitted a tiny shock when she got too close to the boundary of the back yard. Within a few days we realized that she no longer needed the collar. She was conditioned to stay within the borders of the backyard. I'm a bit like

Loodle. When I stray out of the boundaries of my everyday life and receive a little "life shock," I'm loath to repeat the process. As a result, I'm apt to be restricted to the boundaries of my backyard. "Better the devil you know than the devil you don't," goes the old maxim. We seek safety in what we know—the status quo. But unless we risk change, we will never grow.

One of the many things I'm learning later in life is how staying flexible and adaptable to change can enrich my life. When I am poised to take advantage of whatever may present itself in that moment, my life becomes much larger and grander. When I was in Brazil visiting the healer named "John of God," I was fortunate to spend some time with the administrator of his ministry. He told me that John of God was constantly changing policy and procedures as he receives divine guidance. The administrator shared, "It drives us crazy, but I have to admit it also has been very effective. Because we are constantly changing, we haven't been able to settle into the rites, roles, and rituals of many traditional churches. This has allowed us to be more responsive to our constituents' needs, and that is ultimately why we are here."

Gift: Connection

Finally, the gift of Path Two is connection. In today's world we not only crave connection, we crave authentic connection. Think of a time you met someone who struck you as phony. Did you feel connected with him or her? Of course not! Now remember meeting someone with whom you felt authentically connected? It's totally different, isn't it? When we move from our defended to our authentic selves, we forge true, authentic connections. We meet face-to-face rather than mask-to-mask.

Around the time of my divorce, I began seeing a therapist for the first time in my life. After several sessions the therapist suggested that I consider group therapy. I thought to myself, it's bad enough that I'm seeing a therapist (in my family seeing a therapist was considered a form of weakness), but now he wants me to go to group therapy too! But at that point I was willing to do most anything to relieve the emotional pain I was feeling, so I agreed to go. I showed up to the first session to find six losers sitting around in a circle whining about their insignificant lives. After the fourth meeting, one piped up and suggested that I should leave the group. "Me?" I was indignant. After all I was the only one who had it together. Why should I be the one to leave the group? "Week after week we share our lives and our feelings," he continued, "and week after week you share only the facts of your life. If you are experiencing a problem, you always have the solution. You're all persona. We don't have any idea who you really are."

His words stung, but they delivered an epiphany. If I was doing this in this group, I was also doing it with everyone in my life. If I truly wanted to connect with people, I had to learn to become more vulnerable. After accepting my apology, the group allowed me to stay, and I began to slowly share my inner thoughts and feelings. My friends called it "the great awakening." They were right. My entire way of relating to people changed. Stripped of all masks, I was vulnerable, and I was more real. People could relate to me, and I could relate better to people. I became a better manager and a better salesman, co-worker, friend, brother, and person.

We've talked a lot about the defended and the authentic selves. We've discussed how the defended self works, reviewed Kingma's six life themes, and listed a number of attributes of the authentic self. You've learned that the central task of Path Two is to know one's true self, and we've reviewed seven strategies to assist you. We've also reviewed the guide, courageous self, chief obstacle, status quo, and the gift of connection on this path. I'd now like to share a story.

CHAPTER TWENTY-EIGHT

Epiphany on Path Two

For several years now, I've had a recurring dream where I'm working for a public relations agency. I'm not being paid, and I have little to do. The job is pretty much a scam. I go to work every day in order to look good to the outside world. In the dream I know I should quit, but I'm afraid. I'm not sure that I could get a "real job," and what would I do with my time if I no longer have an office to go to?

As dreams do, this dream parallels my waking life. For the past few years I've been winding down my training and coaching practice, and in doing so I've been experiencing a bit of an identity crisis. Without my job, who am I? I already knew this dream was about my fear of losing my identity and having time on my hands, but this dream was trying to teach me something that I didn't already know. I seemed to be eluding its message—otherwise it wouldn't keep repeating itself. I decided to explore this further through active imagination.

Carl Jung first used the term "active imagination" in 1935 to describe a technique that is one of the oldest forms of meditation. It has been used for ages as a way to know God, the Buddha mind, or gods and goddesses. It is also an excellent tool for interpreting dreams. Edward F. Edinger is a founding member of the Carl G. Jung Foundation for Analytical Psychology in New York and the author of numerous books on Jungian psychology. He describes active imagination as "a process in which the imagination and the images it throws up are experienced as something separate from the ego—a 'thou' or 'other'—to which the ego can relate and with which the ego can have a dialogue."

There are many ways to engage in active imagination, including art, movement, and writing. While I've experimented with many of these, my preferred method is to write a dialogue between myself and a character from a dream, or between myself and an aspect of myself, such as fear or my defended self.

I used active imagination to reenter the recurring dream about the public relations job. I dialogued with my fear around the possibility of resigning from my faux job, and through this process I uncovered an important insight. This dream was about feeling unworthy. Do you remember that I wasn't being paid in the dream? Also my skills weren't being utilized. This was all about worth or the lack thereof.

As a child, I didn't feel loved for who I was. I felt like "The Bad Seed," and in order to be loved, I adopted the image of "The Golden Boy." As I dug deeper, I began to realize that not only did I feel unworthy of my parents' love, I also felt unworthy of God's love. Allowing this to sink in, I felt sadness, followed by shame and emptiness. These were feelings that I've spent a lifetime avoiding. I feared that if I really felt them, they would consume me. I actually felt they'd obliterate me.

Most of us hide behind our stories and the identities these stories form in an attempt to defend ourselves against feelings that seem too all consuming to face. In order to become our most authentic self, we must face the abyss of our fear, uncertainty, and loss, and reclaim essential aspects of our being, including those emotions that were too scary to face in the past. I now know it's time for me to acknowledge my basic goodness, and in doing so acknowledge that I am worthy of love—just as I am.

"But how do I do this?" I asked my divine self. I paused, took a deep breath, and began writing all that popped into my head. Here's how my divine self responded: "Don't underestimate the power of awareness. Now that you've recognized that you've felt unworthy of love—even God's love—you can change that. Sit with it, let it simmer, and allow God to come to you. There's nothing for you to do—no magic key will open a hidden door and no genie is coming out of a bottle. Your only task is to be receptive—allow, and above all trust. You are healing even as you write this."

CHAPTER TWENTY-NINE

Tools, Practices, and Questions

I'll share one tool and a practice that I've found particularly helpful on my journey on Path Two. I think you'll be particularly interested in the questions that I included at the end of this chapter, and again I encourage you to explore at least a few that resonate with you.

Tool: Core Values

Earlier we talked about how identifying your core values can help you discover what really matters to you so that you can be your most authentic self. Here's a simple exercise that I offer in my book *Engineer Your Career: Build Your Best Self Blueprint*.

Below you'll find a partial list of values. Are there others you'd like to add to this list? If so, add them. Then circle the values that are very important to you. Can you narrow your life to four or seven core values?

Sample Values

Authenticity	Knowledge	Creativity	Faith
Love	Relationships	Community	Excellence
Justice	Peace	Equality	Communication
Honesty	Kindness	Generosity	Loyalty
Success	Courage	Growth	Wisdom
Integrity	Tolerance	Commitment	Fun
Spirituality	Optimism	Philanthropy	Freedom
Friendship	Empathy	Wealth	Beauty
Security	Adventure	Happiness	Health
Warmth	Good Deeds	Devotion	Connectedness
Service	Appreciation	Ethics	Family
Morality	Innovation	Control	Accuracy
Achievement	Risk	Belonging	Competition
Duty	Fame	Harmony	Independence
Power	Status	_____	_____
_____	_____		

Of these, my core values are (list four to seven):

1. _____   2. _____

3. _____   4. _____

5. _____   6. _____

7. _____

Core Values Litmus Test

Answer these four questions to ensure that these are truly your core values.

1. Value? Is your money where your mouth is? Are you dedicating money and time to the value?
2. Consistent? Do people associate you with this value? Or is it a stretch?
3. Energy? Do you experience excitement, emotion, and energy around the value?
4. Stress? What happens when the chips are down? Do you rely on the core value when you are under stress?

Over the years, I've narrowed my core values to four, all of which begin with the letter "C":

1. Courage
2. Connection (to self, others, and the Divine)
3. Contribution
4. Curiosity

Would you like to take this exercise a little deeper? The chances are the exercise you just completed reflects your *aspirational* core values—those core values that you'd like to list as what guides your life in a perfect world. That's great and certainly valuable to identify, but let's take a candid look at how you live your life. What core values are truly guiding you? Be totally honest. I did and came up with seven:

1. Productivity   2. Service   3. Insight
4. Seduction   5. Recognition   6. Love   7. Beauty

Next I determined which of these core values belonged to my defended self and which belonged to my higher self. Productivity, seduction, and recognition belonged to my defended self, while the remaining four were more indicative of my higher self.

I then took a closer look at the defended self's three core values. I quickly realized that I valued them only because they helped me project an image, and that image did not reflect my most authentic self. In fact, that image was preventing me from being more authentic and connected in my life. As a result of completing this exercise, I've become more alert to when these three core values are at play. When this does happen, I catch myself and change what I was about to say or do because it would reflect a core value that I don't want to identify with.

Practice: Making Peace with Your Past

John Bradshaw has been called "America's leading personal growth expert." The author of five *New York Times* best-selling books, including *Homecoming: Reclaiming and Healing Your Inner Child*, Bradshaw teaches that many of the beliefs that hold us back from becoming our most authentic self are rooted in childhood.

For some, the scars that form those beliefs are deep. A dear friend of mine was sexually abused as a child. She still feels shame and guilt. For others, the scars are not as deep but they are still painful. "I grew up with an older brother who was our family's superstar," a client shared. "He was a great student, athlete, and popular with all the girls. I shriveled in his shadow."

Bradshaw believes that we continue to see the world as a little child—our inner child. Regardless of how mature, powerful, and successful we think we are, that inner child's grief, vulnerability, pain, shame, and anger continue to influence our life. He goes as far as to write, "I believe that this neglected, wounded inner child of the past is the major source of human misery."

But all is not lost, Bradshaw teaches. We can learn to re-parent ourselves and soothe and heal that inner child by giving her what she is longing for. He writes, "Three things are striking about inner child work. The speed with which people change when they do this work; the depth of that change; and the power and creativity that result when the wounds from the past are healed." Most of us still carry around scars from our childhood.

Ask yourself: What are some of yours? What is it that your inner child wants or needs most from you?

Bradshaw believes that as adults, we now have the power to love and nurture our inner child in those ways we craved as children. What is it that your adult self would like to say to your inner child? Some examples include:

- I love you, I care about you, and I accept you just the way you are.
- I am so proud of you and all that you are.
- You are so beautiful and attractive (bright and talented, artistic and creative, etc.)
- I am with you now, and you are safe. You can trust me to take care of you.
- We will work at getting healthy together.

Questions

I've listed seven questions that may be helpful as you explore Path Two in your journal. Again select those that carry the most energy for you.

1. Who is living the life I most envy and why?
2. What would I tell young people are the most important things in life?
3. What did I feel called to do but never acted upon?
4. What needs to be honored in my life? What areas of my life are being neglected right now?
5. What is waiting to die within me? What is waiting to be born?
6. Do I feel I lack permission to be who I am? If so, whose permission am I seeking?
7. In what areas were my mother and father stuck, and how do those issues show up in my life?

As the authentic self matures, it eventually comes to know the higher self. On Path Three we transcend all selves—even the highest one—to become divine, or no self. It's here that we have the potential to discover the "peace that passes all understanding" when all longing ceases.

SECTION VI

Path Three: Higher to Divine Self

Love Dogs
Rumi

One night a man was crying Allah! Allah!
His lips grew sweet with praising,
until a cynic said, "So!
I've heard you calling out, but have you ever
gotten any response?"

The man had no answer to that.
He quit praying and fell into a confused sleep.

He dreamed he saw Khidr, the guide of souls,
in a thick, green foliage.
"Why did you stop praising?"
"Because I've never heard anything back."
"This longing you express
is the return message."

The grief you cry out from
draws you toward union.

Your pure sadness
that wants help
is the secret cup.

Listen to the moan of a dog for its master.
That whining is the connection.

There are love dogs
no one knows the names of.

Give your life
to be one of them.

A Different Reality

Some years ago, through a series of synchronicities, I found myself participating in an Ayahuasca ceremony. For those of you who don't know, Ayahuasca is a hallucinogenic brew made out of the *Banisteriopsis caapi* vine that is used as traditional spiritual medicine among the indigenous people of Amazonian Peru. Spiritual seekers around the world who participate in these shamanistic rituals report visions that can help them cure emotional wounds, find their purpose in life, and experience the truth of the universe.

At the ceremony, I dressed all in white and was seated on the hard wooden floor surrounded by pillows. A blue plastic bucket was placed next to me in case I threw up. I found my mind racing as the Peruvian shaman chanted over the bottle of thick brown Ayahuasca tea. "What in the hell are you doing, Randy?" I berated myself. I hate drugs, and I also hate the feeling of losing control. "What have you gotten yourself into?"

Looking back over that experience, I'm glad I did it. I wouldn't recommend it to anyone else—and I'm certainly not recommending it for you, but for me it was life changing. For the first time, I was able to experience the world without the governor, filter, or damper that my ego places on my senses to "protect me." The world literally came alive. I still wonder today if that's not the way the world really is, but I block myself from seeing it in all its glory for fear of becoming overwhelmed.

I did not lose control, and unlike most of my fellow participants I didn't vomit. My observer self was fully awake witnessing each unfolding scene and grounding the experience in reality. Not only did I get a sense of what it's like to fully experience all five senses, but I also felt as if I had tapped into the collective unconscious. I felt one with everyone and everything around me. Finally I could allow my experience to flow freely through me without feeling a need to cling onto the feeling. My experience with Ayahuasca opened me to the possibility of a different reality than I experience most days—a reality where the ego is not needed to protect me, and the boundaries between this world and other worlds blur to become one.

In this section, we'll meet the higher self and learn that when we evolve from higher to divine self, we transcend the ego to become essence. We'll list the many names for divine self and review the attributes for it. We'll hear how some describe the experience of operating from their divine selves, and learn a new way of serving that is based more on being than doing. We'll learn about the long and short paths to enlightenment and how most of us only get glimpses along the way, but how these glimpses transform us. I'll share seven insights we gain on the long path, and as in the other sections we'll review the guide, chief obstacle and the gift for Path Three. Finally, we'll conclude with several tools, practices, and questions that will assist us along this path.

CHAPTER THIRTY

Meet the Higher Self

The higher self is a term that is used by multiple belief systems, although I've heard it most associated with the New Age movement. While some use the terms higher and divine selves interchangeably, I see them as quite different. When we evolve from our higher to our divine self, we transcend self all together—operating entirely from essence. This is what I believe it means to be enlightened. We'll explore the divine self more in the next chapter. For now, let's return to the higher self.

In his poem, *Promise Yourself,* Christian B. Larson beautifully describes the promise we make when we decide to operate from our higher self.

Promise Yourself

To be so strong that nothing
can disturb your peace of mind.
To talk health, happiness, and prosperity
to every person you meet.

To make all your friends feel
that there is something in them
To look at the sunny side of everything
and make your optimism come true.

To think only the best, to work only for the best,
and to expect only the best.
To be just as enthusiastic about the success of others
as you are about your own.

To forget the mistakes of the past
and press on to the greater achievements of the future.
To wear a cheerful countenance at all times
and give every living creature you meet a smile.

To give so much time to the improvement of yourself
that you have no time to criticize others.
To be too large for worry, too noble for anger, too strong for fear,
and too happy to permit the presence of trouble.

To think well of yourself and to proclaim this fact to the world,
not in loud words but great deeds.
To live in faith that the whole world is on your side
so long as you are true to the best that is in you.

As our higher self, we tap into higher emotions such as love, empathy, and gratitude. A banner hangs in my church in Asheville, North Carolina that quotes spiritual leader Meister Eckhart: "If the only prayer you say in your whole life is 'thank you' that would suffice." Several years ago I began the practice of ending each day listing three things (or people) for which (or whom) I am grateful. I find it the perfect way to end the day and transition to dream time.

According to the law of attraction, we attract that on which we focus. When my thoughts dwell on what I don't have in my life, I attract unsettling feelings of need. The tapes in my head start to whine, "You are not enough. There's not enough." But when I shift my focus from what I don't have to what I do, the tapes stop and beautiful music fills my ears. I am learning to seek gratitude in every situation, even those that I once considered "bad." Dr. Wayne Dyer, in his book *The Power of Intention: Learning to Co-create Your World Your Way*, wrote, "To connectors, everything that shows up in their life is there because the power of intention intended it there. So they're always in a state of gratitude. They feel thankful for everything, even things that seem to be obstacles… Through their thanks, they honor all possibilities.…"

When we are our best selves living our best lives, we are operating from our higher self. We ask ourselves, "Is this in the best interest of me and the Universe?" before embarking on any important task. The higher self is our moral compass. It's guided by our core values and sense of purpose, and above all it is guided by love.

The higher self connects heart to heart and soul to body. We recognize that God is in everyone we meet and everything we see. We hold the delicate balance between loving people for who they are, flaws and all, and supporting them to act from their higher selves. And because we can do this for others, we begin to do this for ourselves.

It's how we express our divinity and authentic selves in the world. Where the authentic self is about being, the higher self is about doing. Higher self is about service or contribution. Its being informs its doing. It's how your soul expresses itself on the earth plane. With a clear sense of purpose or mission, we eagerly put our talents and treasures to work in the world.

CHAPTER THIRTY-ONE

Meet the Divine Self

As your higher self, our personality is fully developed, integrated, and evolved. It may seem that when we're operating from our higher self, our journey to wholeness is complete, but our spirit knows better. It knows we long for nothing less than absolute union with the divine. As we discussed earlier, even when we operate from our higher self, we still are operating primarily from ego rather than essence. And no matter how much we spiritualize the ego, it's still the ego. When we evolve into our divine selves, we leave the ego behind, totally identifying with and operating from essence. When we travel the path from higher to divine self, we follow the examples of Buddha, Krishna, Mohammed, and Jesus, by shifting the "I" of our identity from self to God. In short, we claim our divinity.

There's an eternal spark within us all, and it's our divinity. The more we attend to that spark, the greater the flame will grow, until our whole beings are surrounded by light and all who come into contact with us are warmed by the glow of unconditional love. When we begin Path Three, we acknowledge this spark and commit to attending to it.

Coming from the Christian tradition, I see Jesus as an example of the divine self, and I see his life as a metaphor for the highest spiritual teaching—unconditional love. I believe Jesus did not call us to worship him, but to follow his example and transcend ego, claim our essence, and become channels of divine love. Jesus taught that we have a choice. We can continue to operate from our ego, including our unconscious and defended selves, and live in a world of separation, suspicion, self interest, self protection, lack, fear, and suffering. Or we can claim our birthright and create a world of union, trust, selflessness, service, abundance, love, and peace. The choice is ours, and the self determines which we choose to rule our lives.

Another name for the divine self is no self. The observer self observes; there is a subject who sees an object. Thus it stands to reason that the observer is separate from the object. The divine, or no self, doesn't notice any distinction between itself as the subject and the object it is observing. They are the same. This is what is truly meant by at-one-ment, or "All One."

This concept can frighten us. It certainly does me. Seeing everything as a separate object invites me to conceptualize, name, label, identify, or reify it, and in so doing objectify my world. To my fragile ego, if my world is concrete, then it's real; and if it's real, then I have some control over it.

In his book *The Unfolding Now: Realizing Your True Nature through the Practice of Presence,* A.H. Almaas explains: "Because for us to orient ourselves, to feel a sense of reality, to operate, we feel that we need a foundation, a solid center, a base of operation." He goes on to write, "…we are desperate to have a ground, a center to function from—which ultimately means having a self." Essentially we are looking for validation that we exist. Why? We are afraid of being sucked into the black hole of "the void." Almaas writes, "We are continuously trying to create solidity, because if we let ourselves relax, we will find out that the nature of presence itself is completely, absolutely nothing—it is more nothing than the nothing of empty space. It is nonbeing itself." So it stands to reason that if we demolish this foundation of our sense of reality as we would in a state of non-being, then the world as we know it would crumble. And that frightens us.

Attributes and Experiences of the Divine Self

When we operate from our divine self, we experience unity, insight, and love. We may also feel:

- Crystalline clarity
- Commonality and coherence
- A sense of belonging
- Surreality
- Self-transcendence
- Intimacy
- Safety
- Transformative learning
- Calm and serenity
- Energy and exhilaration
- Focus
- Power and strength

Most report intense feelings of joy, awe, serenity, empathy, compassion, gratitude, and above all, unconditional love. Many report a heightened sense of touch, sound, and sight. Some say they feel as if they are expanding—physically, emotionally, psychologically, or spiritually. Most say they experience such physical sensations as chills, tingling, tears, and pauses in their speech. When I feel particularly connected with the divine, I get goose bumps that I call "God bumps."

Most of us may never experience it, but if we are lucky we may get glimpses—or what the Zen Buddhists call "Kensho"—along the way. What is the experience of no self like? While it's impossible to put such experiences into words, some have tried. I found the insights of Tom Robbins, Carrie Triffet, Bill Walz, and Ralph Waldo Emerson particularly helpful. These writers have found a way to wrap words around an experience that in many ways is indescribable. I am grateful to them and their literary artistry. While I've experienced glimpses of my divine self, I couldn't begin to describe my experience as eloquently. Let's read about what each has to say about the experience of divine or no self.

Tom Robbins shares his experience as only he can in his memoir *Tibetan Peach Pie*. Robbins had just seen Natalie Wood in the film *Tomorrow is Forever* when:

My sorrow unexpectedly widened and deepened, became less focused on the Natalie Wood character, become increasingly comprehensive—enveloping not only hurt children and suffering innocents everywhere but also Hiroshima victims, Huck Finn's Jim, our neighbor's recently euthanized cat, and so on and so forth. Natalie's character also embodied a stubborn, contagious hopefulness, and in me that hope commenced to expand geometrically, as well, eventually morphing into something akin to universal love.

My scruffy whippersnapper heart opened like a sardine tin, my impressionable kiddish brain sidestepped the domination of cognitive experience; I sensed the world in me and me in the world, felt fundamentally connected, saw the many as all and the all as one, one and all bobbing along forever and ever in an unending, indestructible river of tears and tickles, breath and meat. In this totally unfamiliar oceanic state, momentarily free of self-involvement, conventional knowledge, and pedestrian consciousness, radiating such a cortex of woo-woo love it would have made Saint Francis of Assisi seem like a mink rancher....

In her book *The Enlightenment Project,* Carrie Triffet describes no self this way: "…you're not the individual person you thought you were, living inside a body and bound by the laws of time and space. You realize you are none of those things. You're everyone and you're everything. And no one and nothing. You're simultaneously everywhere and nowhere, eternally. You *are* eternity itself."

Bill Walz has a private practice in Asheville teaching meditation and mindfulness. He also writes a monthly article, "Artful Living," for Asheville's *Rapid River Arts and Culture* magazine. In one article entitled "Behead Yourself," he shares this quote from Douglas Harding, *On Having No Head*:

> "It was as if I had been born that instant, brand new… there existed only the Now… It took me no time at all to notice that this nothing, this hole where a head should have been, was no ordinary vacancy, no mere nothing…. Here it was, this superb scene, brightly shining in the clear air, alone and unsupported, mysteriously suspended in the void… utterly free of 'me,' unstained by the observer. Its total presence was my total absence."

> "It can happen in ordinary moments in everyday life when a sudden clarity occurs. It might be stimulated by the sight of birds flying, children playing, the sound, or feel of the wind. You perceptually step out of being separate from what you are experiencing and become the act of seeing, hearing, feeling, experiencing. Thought stops. The usual sense of being a separate self, called 'me,' evaporates. However, because the sense of 'me' evaporates, there is no intellectual 'me' to notice, evaluate and integrate the experience. There is just this experience of fullness, completeness that is inexplicable. Then—it passes. We come back to body and mind, to 'me,' to our 'head.' The moment may go completely unnoticed as anything special, for we are programmed by our society not to notice such occurrences or inquire into their meaning and implication."

Ralph Waldo Emerson wrote in his journal, "The highest revelation is that God is in every man." And in his essay *Nature*, he recounts a transcendental experience: "Standing on the bare ground, my head bathed by the blithe air, and uplifted into infinite space, —all mean egotism vanishes. I become a transparent eye-ball. I am nothing. I see all. The currents of the Universal Being circulate through me; I am part or parcel of God."

The four writers suggest that our concept of self is just that, a concept; it doesn't reflect reality. Instead, it's a series of attachments that we've hung onto to give our psyche structure and give us a false sense that we can control our external world. It's been reported that when no self is experienced there is no sense of "I." There's no sense of separateness. It's as if the self dissolves and only love and light remain, not unlike a single drop of rain falling into the ocean. And again, this frightens us. To give up the outer ego can feel like giving up—while being consumed by—all of existence.

CHAPTER THIRTY-TWO

The Evolution from the Higher to the Divine Self

I need to make a confession: few things give me the creeps more than when someone claims that he or she is enlightened. Enlightenment, as I understand it, is the absence of the one who cares about being enlightened. And I have to be honest, as much as these "enlightened" men and women creep me out, they also inspire me. I think if they can do it, then so can I.

Long and Short Path to Enlightenment

It's been said that we can take two paths to enlightenment: the short or the long path. In our "Just take a pill" culture of instant gratification, most of us prefer the short path. On the short path we pick the winning lottery ticket. In an instant, we become one with God. All the obstructions and obstacles that are in the way of knowing, experiencing, and operating from essence vanish, and we know and identify with our divine self.

One of the better-known short path stories is that of the apostle Paul on the road to Damascus, as told in Acts 9 in the Bible. Saul is walking down the road with a letter in his pocket from a high priest in the temple authorizing him to arrest anyone following Jesus. Suddenly a light from heaven surrounds him. He falls to the ground when a voice calls out, "Saul, why do you persecute me? I am Jesus, whom you are persecuting." From here the Bible gives two accounts as to what happened next. In Acts, Saul becomes Paul and goes on to preach the gospel. His conversion is pretty immediate. Yet in his letter to the Galatians, Paul gives a different account. After meeting Jesus on the road to Damascus, he travels to the desert in Arabia where he spends as much as seventeen years integrating this experience and learning more about Jesus.

My point is this: it's rare that one becomes his or her divine self in an instant. For most of us, Path Three is not so much an event as it is a process—one that evolves over a lifetime (or many lifetimes) and after significant study, discipline, and practice. In truth we are already there. We are already our divine selves—our consciousness is one with source. As Indian yogi and mystic Sadhguru explains, "...it takes time because you do not give in all at once; you give in by installments. So whether you want to go by small installments and take one hundred lifetimes, or you want to do it today is your choice. How long it takes simply depends on how intense is your longing to know."

Again we get momentary glimpses of the God essence within us and the realization that we are all one, but all too soon the ego wields its long sword of fear and these slices of heaven plummet back to the earth. Over time with repeated introspection, study, meditation, and prayer, we are able to strengthen our resolve, weaken habitual patterns, and spend more time in communication and communion with the divine.

We hate to wait. We want it IMMEDIATELY! Yet looking over my life, I've found some compelling reasons why waiting can actually be a good thing. Waiting creates value. We tend to value things more when we have to wait for them. Secondly, waiting helps our intentions and motivations to become clearer. Our motives for wanting something in our life are often mixed, and at times they are at odds with one another. Over time and with perspective, we become able to identify multiple motives and sort through priorities. Finally, waiting allows us to ground ourselves intellectually, emotionally, spiritually, physically, and energetically to be better prepared to receive and retain the full gift of what is being offered.

We've discussed the evolution from higher to divine self as well as the short and long path to enlightenment. Now, let's review seven lessons that we're likely to encounter on the long road to enlightenment.

Seven Lessons for the Long Path

Most of us will take the long path of Path Three. While each journey is unique, we will most likely experience seven common lessons on our way.

Lesson One: We place our identity ("I"dentity) on our divinity.
Lesson Two: We acknowledge that we are all one.
Lesson Three: We are totally present.
Lesson Four: We relax into the silence.
Lesson Five: In acceptance, we find peace.
Lesson Six: We embrace mystery and ambiguity.
Lesson Seven: We become channels of God's love.

CHAPTER THIRTY-THREE

Place Your Identity on Divinity

We've discussed the importance of placing the "I" of our identity on our divinity. When we devote all of our attention to our divine self—its remembrance, various aspects, or the idea of it—we forget ourselves. Only then is it possible to transcend the ego and the physical world and tune into the eternity and the immune core of our being, or our essence. I want to be clear—I'm not saying that we are God. I'm simply saying that we are an expression of God. Dr. Wayne Dyer uses a wonderful analogy of the ocean. He says to imagine the ocean is God. If you take a glass of water from the ocean, it is still an element of God, maybe not as big or powerful, but God nonetheless.

Like Dr. Dyer, I believe there's something bigger than us, and that something is within us. From sacred to secular, many of the world's great teachers have reminded us that God is within—we have only to look to our souls. Whether you call it universal consciousness, Brahma, Buddha nature, or Christ consciousness, it's not something to be achieved; it is a realization of who we are. In Luke 17:21, Jesus says, "For indeed, the kingdom of God is within you." Buddhists believe all beings contain a spark of divine light, and Jewish mystics use similar wording when they talk of the inner spark or the spark of God. The Koran mentions the candle flame burning in a niche in the wall of God's temple when referring to man. A spiritual search is a search for divine or sacred light within us. By cultivating our inner core, we find this light as we come face to face with our own divinity.

German theologian, philosopher, and mystic Meister Eckhart once wrote, "God does not ask anything else of you except that you let yourself go, and let God be God in you." If you are like me, this can be a hard pill to swallow. Heck, it's hard enough for me to take a compliment. Can you imagine how hard it is to accept that I am divine? That would mean I am perfect as I am. Me? I am flaw-filled and full of shame. Just as I accept that God is mysterious and unknowable, perhaps I can also accept that God's infinite love for us reaches beyond the limited comprehension of my tiny brain.

In his *New York Times* bestseller *The Untethered Soul: The Journey Beyond Yourself*, Michael A. Singer explains that it's not as hard as we may think: "Fortunately, deep within us, there is a direct connection to the Divine. There is a part of our being that is beyond the personal self. You can consciously choose to identify with that part rather than with the psyche or body. When you do this a natural transformation begins to take place within you."

CHAPTER THIRTY-FOUR

Acknowledge that We Are One

Lesson two is "We acknowledge that we are one." As divinity, we know in our deepest of hearts that we are one with everyone and everything in creation. We come from the same source—we are made from the same energy. Dr. Wayne Dyer explains, "So when you read about people like Gandhi, Maharaj and Jesus, and people like Ramana Maharshi and Ramakrishna, Mohammed and so on, they're called non-dual beings, people who have 'transcended.' Like it says in the *Bhagavad Gita*, 'they've gone beyond the duality of the physical plain.' So that there's no up and down, right or wrong, beginning and end, rich and poor—there's none of that. There's just this ONE."

To travel Path Three we have to be willing to strip ourselves of the illusion that we are separate. We have to become a part of the collective whole. There are times when I'm giving a workshop that I get a glimpse of this. At those times I lose all sense of self and become one with the audience. I find that when I communicate from this divine place, people listen. They are open and responsive to what I have to say because they intuitively feel—whether or not they are conscious of it—that I love them.

Being one is not about isolation, solitude, or aloneness. Becoming one is a cosmic event as Piero Ferrucci illustrates in his book, *The Power of Kindness: The Unexpected Benefits of Leading a Compassionate Life*. He shares the beautiful Jewish story of a good king who is dying. Before his weeping subjects he calls for an arrow and asks the weakest of them to break it. A frail man steps forward and does so with ease. The king then asks for the strongest of them to break a bundle of arrows bound together. Despite all the strongest man's efforts, he cannot do it. The king says to his subjects, "As my legacy, I bequeath to you the union among you all. Be united with one another. This oneness will give you great strength, which alone you would never be able to attain."

In this age of individualism, perhaps we are missing the gift of our inheritance, which is our unity. When we recognize we are all one, we lead stronger, kinder, and more fulfilled lives. Poetess Annie Besant shares this cosmology:

> O hidden life vibrant in every atom;
> O hidden light shining in every creature;
> O hidden love embracing all in oneness;
> May each who feels himself as one with thee;
> Know he is therefore one with every other.

Judgment and Unity Consciousness

"Boy, aren't you the enlightened one?" my inner critic hisses. "How inauthentic can you be?" My inner critic has a point. As much as I don't want to admit it, I judge people a lot, and when I do I separate myself from them. If I truly practiced "we are one," I wouldn't be so judgmental. However, I've come to realize that I judge people for those things I most fear. For example, I am quick to judge someone who is overweight. Do you remember that I was a fat kid? Today I may be a thin man, but deep within lurks a fat kid. Since I've been traveling Path Two, I'm able to catch myself more frequently when my defended self takes over—like it did on a trip to St. Martin in the Caribbean.

It's been said that St. Martin has some of the most beautiful beaches in the world, and on one of these beaches, Orient Bay, clothing is optional. Don and I decided to be adventurous and check it out. The first thing that struck me was the number of fat people on the beach. Judge Randy had taken the bench! "It seems that those people who should take off their clothes, don't, and those who shouldn't, do," I cattily remarked to Don. Don, acting as my better half, did not respond. I then caught myself.

In reexamining the scene, I realized that I was also impressed that these men and women were so comfortable with their bodies that they had no qualms about being nude in public. They had much to teach me about body image. Putting my insecurities and fears around my own body aside, I removed my bathing suit and entered the beautiful, pale blue water, grateful for the many teachers who surrounded me. My judgments still can obscure the truth that we are all one, but it's happening less often. Increasingly I catch myself, pause, soothe my defended self, and begin to shift my focus from fear to love.

In many ways, our country and our world have never felt so divided. I find this strange, considering that the ease of travel and the Internet have made us a truly global village. It's not the distance or cultural differences that divide us as much as ideology and dogma. Yet if we look a little closer, we'd see that most of us want the same things. There's a beautiful Sufi parable that illustrates this point:

> *Four people were given a piece of money. The first was a Persian. He said, "I will buy with this some 'angur.'" The second was an Arab. He said, "No, because I want 'inab.'" The third was Turk. He said, "I do not want 'inab,' I want 'uzum.'" The fourth was a Greek. He said, "I want 'stafil.'" Because they did not know what lay behind the names of things, these four started to fight. They had information but no knowledge. One man of wisdom present could have reconciled them all, saying: "I can fulfill the needs of all of you with one and the same piece of money. If you honestly give me your trust, your one coin will become as four; and four at odds will become as one united." Such a man would know that each in his own language wanted the same thing, grapes.*

CHAPTER THIRTY-FIVE

Be Present

While Paths One and Two may address the past and even the future, Path Three only deals with the present. On Path Three, we live in the timeless, futureless, pastless now. The future is imagination, the past is memory, and the only reality is this moment.

Most of the world's religions speak to the importance of living in the moment with full awareness. Zen Buddhism especially is known for its emphasis on "nowness," but Hindu, Taoist, Jewish, Moslem, and Christian teachers also urge us to make the most of every day. God describes himself as, "I AM Who I AM" in Exodus, chapter three. Note that the inscription is in the present tense. That's because God only exists in the present moment. When we are in the present, we are in the presence of God. And in the presence of God, we are in the presence of our divine self.

When Don and I lived at the beach for three months, I'd take my dog Loodle to the ocean to watch the sunrise every morning that I could. The sunrises were stunning. To see them was to see the face of God. But instead of being present and allowing the awe of such great beauty to fill me, I tried to capture the experience with my iPhone. Then I would post the photos to Facebook, eager to see how many "Likes" each photo would receive. I got so caught up in the activity and promise of approval that I lost the precious opportunity to commune with the divine. One morning I explored why in my journal.

As I wrote, I began to realize that I didn't know what to "do" with such beauty, and it was hard to "be" with it because of the emotion it embraced. What frightened me so? Was it that if I totally experienced such beauty, I might become one with it? Herein lay another of those damned growth opportunities. Later I found this beautiful quote from John O'Donohue in his book, *Beauty*: "Neither, it seems can we bear very much beauty. The glimpse, the touch of beauty is enough to quicken our hearts with the longing for the divine. Beauty never finally satisfies though she intensifies our longing and refines it."

Giving myself a break, I realized that by writing about this I was entering Path One and bringing what had been unconscious, conscious. I also realized that I was willing to let go of old patterns and try something new, something that would help me become more my authentic self on Path Two. Finally, I stepped onto Path Three by acknowledging that when I experience such beauty, I am on holy ground. God is here, and by fully embracing this experience, I bow to the divinity in all of creation.

CHAPTER THIRTY-SIX

Relax into Silence and Stillness

The winter solstice is my favorite time of the year. More than Thanksgiving, Christmas, or Easter. The winter solstice takes place on the shortest, darkest day of the year. In the darkness, there are no expectations. There's no one to judge and no one to evaluate. In the darkness, I can finally relax the guard. This is my time, and in the silence and stillness of night I enter the other world where dreams come, images unfold, ancestors and guides visit, and I reconnect with God. I find comfort in the darkness. At the same time I know I must make peace with the light, for real peace and true happiness are found in the balance of the two. I've been asking myself how I can bring more solace to my waking day—how I can bring a piece of the peace I experience during the night to the sunlight. The answer is simple: "Be still and know I am God."

Lesson four is "We relax into silence and stillness." Mother Teresa wrote: "We need to find God, and He cannot be found in noise and restlessness. God is the friend of silence. See how nature—trees, flowers, grass—grows in silence; see the stars, the moon and the sun, how they move in silence.... We need silence to be able to touch souls."

Meister Eckhart agrees: "There is nothing in the world that resembles God as much as silence." And Brunton writes: "The true self of man is hidden in a central core of stillness, a central vacuum of silence."

To find silence we must be still, and to be still we must be silent. According to Paul Brunton in *The Short Path to Enlightenment*, the time will come when it's time to stop striving. To stop, be still, and simply find the place of silence within. He writes, "The greatest advance will be made when they cease holding the wish to make any advance at all, cease this continual looking at themselves, and instead come to a quiet rest in the simple fact that *God is*, until they live in this fact alone. That will transfer their attention from self to Overself (Divine Self) and keep them seeing its presence in everyone's life and its action in every event. The more they succeed in holding this insight, the less will they ever be troubled or afraid or perplexed again; the more they recognize and rest in the divine character, the less will they be feverishly concerned about their spiritual future."

Lama Gendun Rinpoche writes in her sweet poem, *Happiness*:

So, make use of it. All is yours already.
Don't search any further…
Nothing to do.
Nothing to force,
Nothing to want,
—and everything happens by itself.

Teacher and author Tara Brach describes this as the "process of wakeful, profound relaxing." She continues, "We become more at home in awareness than in any story of a self who is falling short or on our way somewhere else. We are at home because we have seen and experienced firsthand the vast and shining presence that is the very source of our being."

These writers, as well as countless other writers, teachers, philosophers, and theologians, agree that there's nothing to search for—what we seek is already here. The object of our quest is within us, not outside of us. Put simply: God is but a breath away. In one breath we can be still, silent, and present, and enter into the presence of the divine. It's in the presence of the divine that we reconnect with our divine self.

The moment we feel anger, anxiety, or irritation, we can be assured the ego has reared its head. When this happens we stop, take a deep breath, and reconnect with the divine. We do this over and over until we find our sweet spot, like the tennis player who hits a ball against the wall for hours until the ball and racket meet in that special place, and he makes the perfect shot.

It's that simple, and it's that complicated. It's that easy, and it's that hard to evolve from our authentic to our divine self. Relaxing in the silence can feel like surrender, and there's nothing that frightens the ego more than losing control. Perhaps you remember the wonderful story about a young man who checks into a monastery, ready to be enlightened yesterday. He asks the abbot, "How long will it take me to be enlightened?" The abbot replies, "About ten years." The young man says, "Ten years! Why ten years?" To which the abbot answers, "Oh, twenty years in your case." The young man asks, "Why do you say twenty years?" The abbot says, "Oh, I am sorry I was wrong…thirty years."

Herein lies the reason why I am not enlightened. My ego self is too afraid of giving up the driver's seat. I want to let go, but my hands grip the wheel like a vice. I remind myself that's okay—for now—and then I repeat this mantra: "Patience, trust, and surrender." Patience has never been one of my virtues. In fact I am one of the most impatient people I know.

There's a folk artist from Georgia, Jake McCord, who used to place pieces of his art in the yard to "season." When collectors would visit and try to buy one of the yard pieces, he would emphatically say, "It ain't ready yet." Increasingly I'm seeing Jake McCord's wisdom. Looking at nature, I see its divine timing. There's a divine timing to life too, and whenever I ignore it I get into trouble. I'm reminded I'm trying once again to be in control. I pause, take a deep breath, reconnect to the divine, and say this silent prayer: "Thy will, not my will be done." Once trust is restored in the divine order, I begin to let go.

In his book *Dancing with the Beloved*, Paul Ferrini writes, "Taoists know that when you let life be, it is thoroughly magnificent. In fact, it's magnificent even when you are trying to control it, but you can't see the magnificence because you are fighting 'what is.'" And underneath all the "what is" is holy hunger, the longing to be reunited with our selves, each other, creation, and God.

CHAPTER THIRTY-SEVEN

In Acceptance, Find Peace

We are imperfect people living imperfect lives, and we must accept this fact if we are ever going to find peace. We know this, but we still seek perfection. It's a paradox: in seeking perfection, we experience imperfection. We try to practice acceptance, but instead we find fault with our experience, and then we beat ourselves up. It's a vicious circle. Again we can tune into our observer self and observe the judgment:

I am trying to accept this, but I have lots of judgment about what's going on, and I'm feeling bad about that. I am judging my judgments.

That's what's happening. It's all right; it's not a problem. It's just what is going on.

This takes the pressure off. The question becomes not so much, "How can I avoid getting upset?" but rather, "How will I react when I get upset?" It's okay that things are imperfect or unfinished. We can be just where we are and observe all attachments, expectations, disappointments, or resistance. We can watch it, experience it, and feel it, but not lose ourselves in any drama.

Once we learn to accept where we are, we may even learn *to love* where we are. And when we can love *where* we are, we can better love *who* we are. That isn't as crazy as it sounds. We may learn to be grateful for whatever circumstance we are in, if for no other reason than its ability to teach us.

One day Don and I had a disagreement, which is especially difficult given our distain of conflict. Somehow I was able to tune into my observer self and notice my discomfort. At the same time, I realized that this was just the kind of opportunity that I had been seeking. This was an opportunity to try a new tactic and reframe the situation. Instead of being triggered, reacting out of fear, and snapping at Don, I could try something different and work hard to understand Don's point of view. After tuning into my observer self, I chose to detach from my defended self so that my divine self could take its rightful place. Instead of reacting defensively, I began to ask Don questions. I found that the better I understood Don's perspective, the more I found compassion. Once Don began to feel heard, his guard lessened. We were then able to reach a compromise that we both felt good about.

CHAPTER THIRTY-EIGHT

Welcome Mystery and Ambiguity

Lesson six is "We welcome mystery and ambiguity." There's a beautiful myth that illustrates the importance of this point. It goes something like this:

> *There was once a princess named Psyche who was so admired for her beauty that none dared to propose to her. Fearing that his daughter would live her life alone, her father asked the great god Apollo for help.*
>
> *Apollo instructed the king to dress his daughter in a mourning dress and leave her on top of a mountain at night. Before dawn a serpent would come and marry her. The desperate king reluctantly obeyed.*
>
> *Shivering from cold and terror, the beautiful princess waited in the dark until she fell asleep. The next morning she awoke in a beautiful palace. Now a queen, she was told she could have anything she wanted. There was only one condition: Psyche must never see her husband's face.*
>
> *Every night her husband came to her, and they would make passionate love. She was happy and content with her life and came to love her husband deeply.*
>
> *From time to time, however, she doubted her happiness remembering that Apollo had said that she would marry a serpent. Finally she could stand it no more; she had to know. One night, while her husband slept, she lit a lantern and held it above her bed. Sleeping next to her was not an ugly serpent, but Eros, a god of incredible beauty.*
>
> *Awakened by the light, Eros left the castle disappointed that his wife could not trust him enough to fulfill his one request.*

Driven by fear, the ego seeks to control through knowledge and understanding. It finds comfort in its ability to name, classify, and list. Essence on the other hand, is comfortable with mystery and ambiguity, using metaphor and symbol rather than words to describe the world. On Path Three, we surrender the need to define the indefinable. We acknowledge that the world is filled with paradox and contradictions, and that truth is often found in the tension of opposites. We welcome ambiguity and mystery. We agree with James Hollis when he writes in his book *On This Journey We Call Our Life: Living the Questions*, "The gods (of our inner and outer worlds) will not be mocked; they have a life, will, autonomy, of their own, and resist our efforts at control." We relax the need to be in control, trusting in a divine order, by saying this simple prayer: "Thy will be done."

Making peace with mystery and ambiguity may bring anxiety, but I'll gladly take it over depression. Hollis reminds us that there's a price to be paid regardless of whether we choose to grow or not. Anxiety, he explains, is the price of growth, and depression is the toll for regression. Even so, the benefits for growth far outweigh any anxiety that might arise. "If we befriend the mystery of the soul," writes John O'Donohue in his book *Beauty*, "then we sense the secret depths to our life. And if we come to trust these depths and realize that here is where the significance of our life dwells, then we come to awaken more and more to our true life."

CHAPTER THIRTY-NINE

Become Channels of God's Love

Earlier we talked about what fueled ego and essence: ego is fueled by fear and essence by love. Since Path Three is the journey to divine self or essence, it would make sense that on Path Three we become channels of God's love. Love is the central message to almost any religion you can name. In *The Seeker's Guide: Making Your Life A Spiritual Adventure*, Elizabeth Lesser writes, "Love is the secret you unmask yourself to find; it is the foundation of the spiritual life, the destination where all roads of the journey lead." Also, Indian spiritual master Sai Baba once said, "The aim of all spiritual practice is love."

Remember that the word love is both a noun and a verb. The noun describes a state of being and the verb an action. The only way to embrace love (noun) is to extend love (verb). If we are living expressions of the divine, then love is the highest way we can express our divinity. Love is infinite—it is not a finite resource. In fact, the more we give it the more we can receive it, and the more we receive it the more we can give it. Love engenders love. Mother Teresa once said, "If you can't do great things, do little things with great love. If you can't do them with great love, do them with a little love. If you can't do them with a little love, do them anyway. Love grows when people serve."

Love and Service

When we are channels of God's love, we seek to serve. Service is a natural expression of love. And when we serve, that love grows. I've mentioned before that I've had the privilege to mentor a number of young people over the past few years. I'm not sure who has gotten more out of these relationships—my mentees or me. Helping these young people identify, name, claim, and express their gifts in the world has brought me great joy and a more open heart.

The connection between love and service is a subject near and dear to the heart of our current pope. Known by some as the "people's pope," *The New York Times* described Pope Francis this way: "He may be the world's foremost Catholic, but to his fans Pope Francis is more like the Reverend Dr. Martin Luther King, Jr. than Pope Benedict XVI. He speaks and millions listen—whether they are Muslim or Baptist, Hindu or atheist." When Pope Francis visited Cuba in 2015, he told the Cuban people that love and service, not ideology, are the keys to their happiness. Love, he said, is lived in a concrete commitment to caring for others—especially the most vulnerable.

Being a man of action, I've always focused on acts of service. Then I stumbled upon this beautiful quote by one of my favorite writers, Ann Lamott, and it helped me see service in a new light: "Lighthouses don't go running all over an island looking for boats to save; they just stand there shining." Lamott's metaphor of the lighthouse blew me out of the water and reframed the way I looked at my life. It helped me see that acting, while important, is not enough. Service that produces real change requires doing *and being*. Eckhart Tolle in *The Power of Now* puts it a bit differently: "But who you *are* is always a more vital teaching and more a powerful transformer of the world than what you say, and more essential even than what you do." Tolle's quote reminds me of a story that proves his point.

After a grueling series of flight delays, I found myself at the Atlanta airport at 5 a.m. As I wearily waited for my next flight, I went to the food court to grab a cup of coffee. Behind the counter, a beautiful heavy-set African-American woman with a one hundred-watt smile greeted me with, "Good morning, honey." She said it in a way that conveyed she really meant it. "How can I help you?" After twenty-four hours of dealing with angry, impatient travelers and war-weary airline personnel, my energy immediately shifted. I gave her my order, and she looked me in the eye again, smiled, and said, "You have a beautiful day!" I was so captured by her warmth, caring, and charisma that I took a seat facing the kiosk and watched her for a while. She met each traveler with equal enthusiasm. A middle-aged white man entered the line and she recognized him. "Hi sweetheart! I haven't seen you in a while," she enthused, and he beamed. One after another she greeted each customer as if he or she was a beloved relative returning home after a long absence. This woman—a total stranger—gave me a great gift that morning. She dissolved my negative attitude and kicked my day off on a positive note. Multiply that by the number of travelers whom she touched that day, and you'll see she made quite an impact. She transformed what would appear to be a menial job into an elegant ministry of love.

Like the lady behind the counter at the airport, we all have the potential to play priestly roles in the lives of those with whom we come into contact every day. It only requires that we take the time to connect and project love. This doesn't mean we have to lose productivity—the woman at the airport quick-service restaurant didn't. She was fast and efficient. But she looked each customer in the eye and was present. She made my day, and I left our momentary encounter dedicated to doing the same for someone else.

Scary Times

We live in scary times, and at no time has the world needed us more. As if acts of terrorism, school shootings, church shootings, the refugee crisis, genocide, disease, hunger, poverty, and global warming aren't enough, what does it take to get our attention? These events may disrupt our lives for a news cycle or two, but all too soon we return to the security of the status quo, justifying our non-action with: "These problems are just too big. What can one person do?"

No longer can I ignore what happens to my brothers and sisters around the world—no longer can I ignore their pain. I can do something. I can vote, protest, write a check, write my congressman, and pen a commentary and post it on Facebook. No act is too small. But to be truly effective, acts must be grounded in love, not fear. I visualize the terrorists. I feel their desperation—their despair. I see them as children—I see their innocence. I seek compassion. I visualize a world where the veils are removed and we see our brothers and sisters for who they are: extensions of us—crafted from the same energy, created from the same source. I take a deep breath and find the stillness. In the stillness I find God.

I begin to blur the man-made lines that divide us—religion, ideology, economics, education, and nationalities. Instead of seeing Isis, Al Qaeda, Russia, and the Religious Right as the problem, I recognize the bigger cause—extremism breeds fear. James Hollis writes in *The Eden Project*, "The power of love is found most in its triumph over fear."

I don't pretend to understand these events, but this I know: Albert Einstein was right when he wrote, "You can't solve problems by using the same kind of thinking we used when we created them." I choose love over fear. The future of the human race depends on me, and it depends on you. Together we have the power to change the world through our actions and the way we choose to live our lives.

My inner critic snickers and once again attempts to throw cold water on my thoughts. Loving others is hard enough when it's someone we like, but loving someone we find difficult can feel impossible. And to be honest, sometimes—no most times—loving myself is hardest of all. "Loving yourself is the greatest work you will do in this life. In a sense it is your only work," Daphne Kingma writes. I read once that we can only love others to the degree we love ourselves. If there's truth in this statement—and I believe there is—then I am screwed. I am extremely judgmental, and I am most judgmental of myself.

CHAPTER FORTY

Love, Judgment, and the Unlovable

I've found a new power word. Using it has helped me connect with and feel love for others—and myself—much more easily. That word is innocence. When we are wounded, we lose touch with our innocence. It doesn't go anywhere—it's a part of our most authentic self. We just lose sight of it. When we become reacquainted with innocence, we begin to reconnect with our essence and the essence of those around us.

I had to take baby steps to get there. While at first I couldn't see others' innocence, I did find it in Loodle when she was a puppy. A year later I found innocence again when I traveled to Africa to volunteer at a school for several weeks. For years I've written "We are all one" and "We are here to love," but it wasn't until I was with the children of Kenya that these abstract concepts came alive. The beautiful ebony faces, innocent eyes, and bright smiles of those children captured me—I fell in love a thousand times over. I never fathered any children of my own, but now I have many. After this incredible experience I began to slowly recognize the innocence in more and more people, even some that in the past I would have deemed difficult to love.

I've found that when people are being difficult, my wounded inner child recognizes theirs and I can find empathy. Marianne Williamson says there's either love or a call for love. I see their less-than-desirable behavior as a call for love. And what's really cool is that I've found that in giving others a break, I'm finally giving myself one.

A while back, I met a friend for a drink. It had been some time since we had last gotten together, and within minutes I remembered why. My friend is self-centered, overconfident, and totally unaware of the impact she has on other people. After a while I gave up trying to share anything about my life. Each time I tried, she would divert the conversation back to her. Her bulletproof confidence bordered on arrogance, shooting holes in whatever likeability or credibility she might have. As my frustration and anger escalated, I asked myself why I was wasting my time with this person. I caught myself. Every situation is an opportunity to learn (Path One). What could I learn here?

My strong reaction required a second look. Could she be reflecting something that I didn't like about myself? I paused and took a deep breath. I had to admit that at times I can be self-centered, and I can get so focused on a goal that I don't see how other people are reacting. Additionally I can appear hyper-confident, especially when I'm feeling insecure. Suddenly instead of anger, I felt compassion—for my friend and for myself. I saw our innocence.

This was a great lesson on the spiritual path. "When we learn to respond to the fear of others in a loving way, we can be sure that our own fears rest in the most compassionate embrace. We are no longer emotional reactive or ambivalent, but patient and steady, knowing that love is real. Everything else is illusion," writes Paul Ferrini in his book, *Return to the Garden*. In the short time I spent with my friend that evening, I learned an invaluable lesson on how to deal with people I find difficult. I can:

1. Focus on my words and actions rather than theirs.
2. Accept that I am them, they are me, and we are one. They are reflecting back a part of myself that I don't like or accept.
3. Realize that when we engage in less-than-stellar thoughts or behaviors, we are coming from fear. I can see their vulnerability and innocence as well as my own.
4. Express true caring and love, knowing that when I do the energy will shift.

In her book *Long Time No See: Diaries of an Unlikely Messenger,* Carrie Triffet sums up this connection beautifully, "Although I think I see you as separate from myself, and although I'm tempted to perceive you as guilty, in reality I'm completely mistaken. I'm not seeing you as you really are. In truth, you are holy and innocent, perfect and pure. You can't possibly have sinned, because sin doesn't really exist. You are divine love, immortal spirit, and you remain exactly as God created you. And you and I are one, eternally safe in Heaven."

You might be thinking, well what about people who are just plain nasty and out to get us? When people strike out against me, I try to see it for what it is: a cry for love. Their intention is not so much to harm me as it is to protect themselves from being hurt. When I see that they are operating from their fear and woundedness, it's easier to find compassion.

Loving the Unlovable

All that said, it's still the case that there are some people who seem just too hard to love. Billy (I changed his name) was one of those. Billy worked for me in the public relations agency that I ran. He was one of my most senior employees, and he did everything in his power to discredit me, accusing me of having no vision and few leadership skills. I was insecure enough that his words stung—even years after I had left the agency.

Since that time, I found a way to make peace with Billy when I finally understood that he had done me a favor: he had helped keep me humble. As one of the youngest general managers of a large public relations agency, I was beginning to believe my own press. Billy helped keep me real and keep my persona in perspective—he was my Auriga. In Ancient Rome, the Auriga was a slave with gladiator status whose duty was to drive a chariot for important military leaders. During the Roman Triumphs, one of his roles was to hold a laurel crown over the head of a military leader while continuously whispering in his ear "Memento homo" or "Remember you are only a man." I am now grateful to Billy for this role he played in my life.

Okay Pollyanna, you may be thinking, but what about when the unforgivable happens? Your best friend has an affair with your husband, or even worse… your child is murdered. Conventional wisdom tells us that we must forgive, but forgiveness may seem impossible. I want to offer another alternative that may feel more doable: we can accept what happened. Bad things *do* happen to good people, and in accepting this truth we can move forward with our lives. We can feel what we feel, including grief and rage, without the need to feel guilty. We can choose not to forgive the perpetrator—for now—leaving open the possibility—no matter how slight—for forgiveness in the future. No balm is more healing than time.

That concludes the seventh and final learning on Path Three. Before moving on, let's review what we've covered so far in this section. We learned that there's a long and a short path to enlightenment. While most of us would prefer the short one, we are unlikely to stumble into a burning bush and become one with the light. Instead we'll most likely find ourselves on the long path. While each of our journeys will be unique, the chances are strong that we'll learn seven lessons along the way:

Lesson One: One hundred percent of our identity ("I"dentity) is placed on our divinity or essence rather than form or ego.
Lesson Two: We acknowledge that we are all one.
Lesson Three: We are totally present.
Lesson Four: We relax into the silence.
Lesson Five: We find acceptance, and in the acceptance we find peace.
Lesson Six: We embrace mystery and ambiguity.
Lesson Seven: We become channels of God's love.

CHAPTER FORTY-ONE

The Guide, Chief Obstacle, and Gift

The guide for Path Three is holy hunger. In Section One we talked about how we long for "*the* One" when really what we want is "*The* One." We discussed that within each of us is a holy hunger—a restless pursuit of "More!" that can only be satiated upon our return to the metaphorical Garden of Eden, referring to our essential connectedness, unity consciousness, or communion with our selves, each other, creation, and God. In Section Three we saw that our lives can be driven by ego or essence, and for most of us the ego takes the wheel most of the time. The ego is never satisfied. Whether it's power and influence, security, or a soul mate that truly hooks us, the ego always cries out for more.

Paths One and Two can't deliver all the love and peace we crave. Our longing will never be satiated until we reunite with our divine selves. I am finding that the deeper I travel down the spirals of the three paths, the more intense this longing for the divine becomes. I understand that this is not unusual. As we travel down to the depths, this holy longing will consume us until we become one with the divine.

Chief Obstacle: The Need to Feel Special

Mystics and poets have written through the ages about our innate need to lose ourselves in order to find ourselves. By that they didn't necessarily mean we were to lose our individuality. Our individuality is crucial if we are to function in the world. Instead, I believe they are suggesting that we lose *our attachment to* individuality with its desires, hates, fears, angers, passions, possessions, foibles, skills, and strengths. In short, the evolution from higher to divine selves requires letting go of the need to feel special. This is a herculean task for many of us, and it's also the chief obstacle along Path Three.

I have a limiting belief that prevents me from living my best life—this belief is "I don't belong." While few would suspect it, most of the time I feel like the odd man out. Because of this limiting belief, there are times when I don't feel connected, and connectedness is a basic human need—just like air, water, and food. I've wondered why I hold onto to the belief. What's the benefit? Perhaps it's that if I don't belong, then I am separate—maybe even unique. In our hyper-individualistic world, being unique is a highly regarded asset. Surpass the ordinary, become extraordinary, and you're a star. You're special.

The defended self teaches us to feel special by being smarter, more beautiful, richer, talented, or even more mischievous or unhappier than others. It promises that if we succeed, we'll win the approval, admiration, and love that we so desperately desire. But being "extraordinary" exacts a great price. Stardom separates us from others, and when we are disconnected from community, our lives are less satisfying. Do you remember the story I told in the last chapter about the friend I met for a drink? She talked non-stop about herself and her accomplishments. In an attempt to be special, she broke her connection with me. How often do I forego connection by trying to impress others with my accomplishments?

On the other hand, am I suggesting that we hide our light under a bushel? Absolutely not! What I've learned is that when my focus shifts from showcasing my skills to using them in the best way possible for the best possible good, I connect with others. When I move from competition to collaboration, my star shines brightest.

I've felt special for as long as I can remember. Maybe it's because I was the youngest child by eleven years or because I grew up with certain social and financial advantages. Whatever the reason, feeling like a standout served me well during the first half of my life. My confidence contributed to a successful career in public relations. In the second half of life, however, this "specialness" became more of a liability. I've come to realize that if I'm special, then I'm separate from others. At this point in my life, connection has become more important to me than career success.

The Gift: Peace

The promise of Path Three is what Philippians 4:7 calls the "peace which transcends all understanding." When we experience such peace, all longing ceases. We are bathed in a soothing presence, and we are completely at rest.

Such peace can only be found in the presence of God. In Isaiah there's a prophecy about the coming Messiah that names Jesus the "prince of peace." Hours before Jesus was crucified he said, "Peace I leave with you; my peace I give you. I do not give to you as the world gives. Do not let your hearts be troubled and do not be afraid." (John 14:27) Later in John, 16:33, Jesus says, "These things I have spoken to you, that in Me you may have peace. In the world you will have tribulation; but be of good cheer, I have overcome the world." Jesus is describing a divinely-inspired inner peace that is not determined by the circumstances of our lives, but rather a state of being deep within us. Like most mysteries, this peace is difficult to define.

The best analogy I know is that of an ocean. On the surface, a storm may be brewing—the waves are rough and the water is turbulent. But deep below the ocean's surface, it's calm. This is what it's like to experience the peace that passes all understanding. Regardless of what is happening in the world around us, deep within we are centered, calm, and tranquil. Enlightened gurus project such peace. We feel bliss by simply being in their presence. Anyone who has heard the Dali Lama speak knows this. In his presence we feel incredible sweetness, boundless love, childlike simplicity, and unbridled joy. Observing these enlightened ones in their different activities, we notice that they flow between being fully present in outer activities and somewhat distant and trancelike when engaged in the inner world.

Recently I read about the life of Claude Monet, the great French impressionist painter. "Let everything about you breathe the calm and peace of the soul," Monet once said. In his later years, his words were put to the test as he faced a series of major trials. When the painter was seventy-one, his beloved second wife died. A few years later his eldest son, only forty-seven, died. Then World War I erupted. All the while his eyesight was failing.

In his late sixties and early seventies the painter could no longer deny that he was going blind from cataracts. Monet's love of light and his lifelong exposure to it had blinded him, and his love of painting had blinded him to his growing blindness. As his sight deteriorated, he painted what he saw—which was diffused and abstract. He underwent a series of glasses, surgeries, and a horrible ordeal with various medicines. At times he lost faith and became discouraged and depressed, but by age eighty-five he again found peace while working on a series of paintings of his garden at Giverny. It was here he painted the famous water lilies, which would become some of his most well-known and beloved paintings. Looking at these lush canvases today, we experience "the calm and peace of the soul."

At this point you may be feeling a bit frustrated, as Path Three may seem quite unattainable. But let me assure you that enlightenment is not an all or nothing thing.

CHAPTER FORTY-TWO

Enlightenment Is Not a Destination

While many have claimed to achieve enlightenment, few actually have reached it. Those who have got there by denying their bodies and the world. They live in seclusion protected by devotees who care for their earthly needs. For most of us, this is not practical—but that doesn't mean that we can't enjoy some of the benefits of enlightenment.

We've heard it said many times, "It's about the journey, not the destination." Nowhere is this truer than on Path Three. When we commit ourselves to this path we will get glimpses of our divine self along the way, and once we have a glimpse one thing is for certain: we've begun to awaken. The process cannot be reversed, but it can be delayed by the ego. About half of Americans claim to have had some kind of mystical or religious experience. Some glimpse their divine selves and panic, then they quickly return to the safety of what they know: identifying with their physical bodies and a separate sense of self. In contrast, others may react by becoming inflated once they can lay claim to being enlightened.

Enlightenment is not a place to reach; it's not a thing to "get," and it's not even an experience. It's the nature of the moment. It's not there—it's here. It's the simple realization that you are divine. It happens when you place 100 percent of your identity on your divinity and by doing so, come into what some have called unity consciousness. Deepak Chopra is one of the world's most recognized teachers about the mind-body connection. He explains that unity consciousness is a state of consciousness where we are constantly tuned into the observer self, or witness. As the observer, we recognize that we are pure consciousness. He shares, "The culmination of enlightenment is the knowledge that consciousness alone exists, that is all there is, was, or ever will be."

So instead of seeking enlightenment, perhaps we should simply strive to honor our self and the no self, our divinity and our humanness, and our unconscious, conscious, defended, authentic, higher, and divine selves. By being in touch with each, perhaps we can attend to daily living while our thoughts, intentions, and actions stay in communion with our divine selves.

The Lesson of the Balance Beam

While Don and I were in St. Simons Island overseeing the renovation of our new home, we hired a physical trainer, and one of the exercises he devised for us was walking on a balance beam. We quickly learned that when we focused on each individual step, afraid we might fall, we would lose our balance, but when we focused on the horizon while visualizing the end of the bar, our feet found their footing and we glided across the bar with grace. Dancing is the same way. When I focus on each individual move, afraid that I'll forget a step, I stumble. But when I allow the music to flow through me, keeping in mind the dance that I am dancing, my feet glide across the floor.

Life is like that balance beam, and it's like dancing. I am at peace when I'm conscious of what I'm feeling in the moment, but not dwelling upon it. By placing my focus on my divine self, I focus on the whole rather than pieces. My divine self is the part of me that is grounded in love, abundance, and union. It's connected with the divine rather than on the "small self" that concerns itself only with petty wants and needs and is motivated by fear, lack, and separation.

But this greater focus on my divine self doesn't mean that I won't have bad days. Job losses, illnesses, disappointments, and disillusionments will come, as will promotions, births, and great gratitude for all. At times I'll feel disappointed, sad, and angry, and when I do I'll try to be with these feelings—but not bask in them, knowing that they will pass in time. Emotions always do. I'll do my best not to let them derail me and break my connection with the divine.

This is most difficult when I am feeling anxious. Anxiety is now the leading emotional disorder in the United States, followed by clinical depression. In today's world most of us are no strangers to anxiety; it acts out in our lives in a myriad of ways, all of which have the capacity to derail us. Recently I realized that I had been shopping more than usual. I seemed obsessed with buying things. Something was off. Curious, I decided to check in with my divine self. I began to write, and this is what came out:

R: I need to talk to you? Are you available?

DS: I'm always here.

R: Thank you for that. I've been noticing that I've been buying stuff a lot. I seem to be a bit obsessed with shopping. I sense I'm doing this to relieve some kind of anxiety. In the past we've identified that these types of behaviors are about avoiding the present moment, but my life seems pretty peaceful right now. I don't think I'm stressed. Am I fooling myself?

DS: Whoa! Let's regroup. Pause a minute and take a deep breathe…. And another…. Scan your body. Can you find any tension?

R: Yes, my shoulders. They are practically at my ears.

DS: Okay. Just notice that. Continue scanning your body. What else do you notice?

R: My stomach is tense.

DS: Good. Just notice that. Continue scanning.

R: My butt is clenched. It's as if I'm holding myself in the chair rather than letting the chair hold me.

DS: Good. What else?

R: Okay, my breath is a bit shallow. I'm breathing from the chest up.

DS: Good. Anything else?

R: That's all I notice right now.

DS: So would you say you are anxious?

R: Yes.

DS: That's good information. Now, what do you remember about anxiety?

R: Anxiety is fear, and fear is the chief motivator of the ego.

DS: Right. So when anxiety shows up that's an indication that the ego has taken over, right?

R: Correct. But why am I anxious in the first place? What in my life has caused this anxiety? And why do I think that buying things is going to relieve that anxiety? Is it because I get a small sense of accomplishment buying something or that I think that whatever I'm buying will help me define myself or build my identity?

DS: Could be that and much more, but do you see that you're starting to fall down a rabbit hole?

R: What do you mean?

DS: Compulsions are almost always a cover for underlying emotions. You are delaying—not avoiding—the real work of being with your emotions and exploring what you are feeling in this moment by going into your head.

R: Wow, you are right. I'm busted. (I laugh.)

DS: So let's put aside what causes it and what will make it go away and return to anxiety through the lens of the three paths.

R: Okay.

DS: You are on Path One. You are working to bring what is unconscious, conscious. At the same time you are also on Path Two; you are observing your defended self and exploring how to become more authentic.

R: And Path Three? The evolution from higher to divine self?

DS: (Laughs) Well, we're talking, aren't we?

R: And that's a start.

DS: Yes it is, and....

R: If anxiety indicates that the ego has taken over, then you are calling me to return home, back to you.

DS: Good. Go on.

R: So the first step is to pause, take a deep breath, and tune into my body. Track sensation.

DS: And why do you do this?

R: Tracking bodily sensations stills my mind and helps me become present.

And in the present I am in the Presence.

DS: Exactly. Go on.

R: I enter the silence and stillness. I go within, and by going within I can connect with you, with my divine self. It's there I find my footing and walk on holy ground.

DS: You are a good student.

R: (Laughs) A slow one. You've been patient. What I'm learning about myself is that I continue to look outside of myself to solve problem and soothe troubled emotions, and that seldom—if ever—works. The answers are within. You are teaching me to live from the inside out rather than the outside in, and the three paths are one way to do that.

DS: Good job! So what are you going to do the next time you have an urge to shop?

R: Pause and reconnect with you.

DS: Good job!

Again, enlightenment is not an all or nothing thing. Almost all of us experience glimpses along the way, and these glimpses awaken us. Maybe instead of seeking enlightenment we should take a step back and remember the lesson of the balance beam: attend to daily living while focusing our thoughts, intentions, and actions on the divine. Most of us will not be able to maintain this state all the time. Anxiety will arise and we will lose our footing, but we regain it by:

1. Exploring why we are employing the ego to protect us. It's most likely based upon an outdated or false fear.
2. Putting the ego to rest by observing our defended self without judgment, becoming aware of thoughts and feelings as they occur and remembering that this awareness allows us to disidentify from our thoughts and feelings.
3. Shifting to our divine self by becoming present and remembering essence can only be found in the present and that one of the best ways to become present is to tune into sensation.

As I did for Paths One and Two, I'll now share several additional tools, practices, and questions that I've found particularly helpful on my own journey.

CHAPTER FORTY-THREE

Tools, Practices, and Questions

Paths One and Two rely more on technique, discipline, and in many cases doing. Path Three is different: it depends more on a way of being rather than doing. Path Three requires us to become receptive channels for God-consciousness. This means becoming truly receptive to the spiritual being within us—that deepest part of our being where the personal self vanishes and nothing can be reflected from the outside world. It's here, Brunton writes, "where God and man may mingle."

Many masters teach that there's no path to enlightenment. There's no need: you are already there. And when we start striving to get there, we're sure to lose our way. We are what we seek to become, we need only to remove the blinders of the ego and recognize our essence, our oneness, our perfection, and our divinity. Put another way, enlightenment is not about becoming something or someone; it's about letting go of what you are not.

Okay, my inner critic chimes in, let's be real—Path Three requires a conscious effort. My inner critic is right in this case. It is important to have a spiritual practice. But don't let the term spiritual practice scare you. A spiritual practice is simply a commitment of how you connect with your divine self. Some people meditate, either by becoming quiet or through body centered meditation such as yoga or dance. Others study spiritual material such as *The Bible, Kabbalah, Gnostic Gospels*, or *A Course in Miracles*. Many seek community with like-minded people either in a church, synagogue, mosque, prayer group, or Bible study. I meet once a week with a dream group. Spiritual practices are personal and unique to each individual.

Paul Brunton writes that in order to be in right relationship with our divine self, we must learn two things: first, how to still our mind; and second, how to place the ego and universe in their proper perspectives. And the two depend on one another.

We've also talked a great deal about how to put the ego and the outside world in perspective by remembering that they are just a small part of what and who we are. Remembering the metaphor of the balance beam, I keep my eye on the bigger picture—on my connection with the divine—rather than the little details of my day-to-day life.

It doesn't make any difference which spiritual practice(s) you choose as long as each helps you remove any obstacles that prevent you from becoming a channel of divine love. For example, I receive the most wonderful lessons in how to love unconditionally through taking care of my dog, Loodle the Poodle. And my relationship with Don has become a part of my spiritual practice. This is important, and I'll talk more about that in the next section. What's important to remember here is that all of these practices require commitment and repetition in order to achieve and maintain a consistent connection with the divine.

I will now highlight four practices that have been meaningful to me.

Practice One: Pray without ceasing.

It's unusual to spot a car in Asheville, North Carolina, without at least one bumper sticker. Folks around here like to make statements, and one of the more popular bumper stickers is one that reads "We Still Pray." I have to confess that I cringed when I first read "We Still Pray." And I know I'm not alone. Prayer can be a loaded word for many of us. When I hear the word prayer, I visualize myself as a child positioned on a hard kneeler in Atlanta's stone Cathedral of St. Philip's reciting monotone prayers containing words I didn't understand and too many statements I did not believe.

As an adult, my feelings around prayer have softened. In the Sufi tradition, there are three ways of communicating with Mystery: prayer, meditation, and conversation. I like using all three. Sometimes I write prayers in my journal or I meditate, but mostly I'm in conversation with God. Normally, it's a casual thing. I'll think, "Thank you God, for this beautiful day." Or, "God, please be with my sick friend." And every now and then, God talks back. A hunch, dream, or synchronicity appears and demands my attention. Sometimes my higher power and I have active conversations. These conversations mostly take place in my journal. Here's how our dialogs go:

RS: God, can we talk?

HP: Of course we can. I've been waiting for you.

RS: Thank you. It's comforting to know you're always there.

HP: You're welcome.

RS: I need your advice on....

HP: What do you think you should do?

RS: Well....

HP: That's one way of looking at it. Have you thought about....

RS: No, but I will. Thank you.

HP: You are welcome.

It's a polite exchange and almost always insightful. Sometimes I'm tempted to ignore my higher power's wise counsel, saying it's just my imagination. Then I have to admit that regardless of where it comes from, it's good advice. I'd be foolish not to pay attention. The older I get, the more I like communicating with my higher power. It's like being with the person who loves you most in the world and always has your best interest at heart.

In 1 Thessalonians 5:17, the Apostle Paul directs us to "pray without ceasing." I believe this means keeping the lines of communication with my higher power open, and that means regardless of whether I'm praying, meditating, or conversing with God—or not—keeping an open heart and a mind fixed upon the divine.

Practice Two: Be still and know I am God.

"Be still and know I am God," the Psalms remind us. When we still the mind, we become present, and when we are present, we are in the presence of God. Eckhart Tolle in *A New Earth* writes: "To be still is to be conscious without thought. You are never more essentially, more deeply, yourself than when you are still.... When you are still, you are who you are beyond temporal existence: consciousness—unconditioned, formless, eternal."

And it scares us to death.

I look at other spiritual seekers only to see myself. They run to this workshop or the next or experiment with one new practice or another, seeking what they already know. What are we running from? Stillness? That's counterintuitive, for it's in the stillness that we will find "it." We will find the core of our being, connection, and communion with the divine, and that peace that passes all understanding. Still it's true—we fear the stillness, and we fear the silence.

Why? According to Bruce Fell, it's because of our culture's constant accessibility and exposure to background media. Fell directed a study of 580 undergraduate students over a six year period, and reported his findings in *The Conversation US,* an independent news source from the academic and research community directed to the general public. This fear of silence is learned and as such can be unlearned.

A while back I attended a weeklong meditation retreat in the mountains outside of Asheville. No meat, no alcohol, and no sex. Seven days of sitting, stillness, and silence. I wasn't sure I could do it—I'm just too hyper. But I did do it, and I actually enjoyed it. I learned that thoughts pop into my mind (Buddhists call this "monkey mind"), and I could simply observe them and watch them pass until the next one appears. It was like standing on a platform at the train station and watching the trains pass by. At times I'd get hooked on a thought and get carried away, but I could catch myself, return to my breath, and once again enter the stillness.

As we discussed earlier, sensation also helps us find stillness. When I tune into sensation I am able to quiet my mind. I sit up straight or I lie down on the floor. Either way my back is supported. I become conscious of my breathing and then start to pay attention to my body.

I can feel the floor supporting my back. Can I release into the floor just a bit more?

I feel the soles of my feet on the floor (My legs are bent.).

The right foot feels a bit heavier than the left.

I also feel where my shoulder blades touch the floor.

I flatten my back, pushing my lower back into the floor. That feels nice.

The air conditioning is blowing on my face. I feel it more on my right side than on the left.

The back of my head….

You get the idea. Tracking sensation is one of the most effective means I know to calm my thoughts and become present. And it's only in the present that I can connect with the divine. From that peaceful posture, prayer naturally emerges. Prayer is my time to communicate with the divine, and meditation is my time to listen. Cistercian monk and priest Thomas Keating says, "Silence is God's first language. Everything else is a poor translation." Also, *Conversations with God* author Neale Donald Walsch writes, "The question is not to whom does God talk, but who listens."

Finally, stilling the mind doesn't have to be a twenty minute procedure. Increasingly I'm finding myself at a traffic light or in the line at the grocery store, remembering that God is only a breath away. I then take a deep cleansing breath and re-connect with the divine.

Practice Three: Split your attention.

The best way I know for keeping the "I" of our identity on the divine is to learn how to split our attention. When we split our attention we fully attend to the outer world while keeping part of our attention on ourselves as we do it. Some call this "self-remembering."

There's a difference between self-awareness and self-remembering. I was reminded of this when I was attempting to explain the concept of split attention to my partner Don. He said he thought he understood. "For example, I'm at a party talking to friends, and at the same time I'm noticing how my interaction is being received by others," he offered. "I see where you're coming from," I said, "but, I don't think that's it." I was at a loss to explain why.

Later that night I thought about it more. When we are *self-aware* we have tuned inward, but the majority of our attention is on the outside world. As Don reminded me, we are scanning our environment to determine how we are being received. As such, the ego is activated because the "I" of our identity is being determined in part by others' reactions to us. When we are *self-remembering* the ego is less involved—if involved at all. We have touched into our divine self; we are conscious of our consciousness, and something deep within informs us that this consciousness is who we are—not our body, roles, thoughts, or feelings. With split attention we are fully engaged in whatever activity we are participating in as well as our internal world. Using Don's example, in a social situation we may experience split attention by being fully present with those with whom we are conversing and at the same time being aware of what we are feeling as we listen and talk.

When I paint I often listen to soft instrumental music. I've found that when I do, I seem to lose myself and go deeper into the process of painting. When I go about my day with the music of "I AM" playing softly in the back of my mind, I am more present and feel more connected with the divine. As a result, my day feels richer. If you're like me, you may split your attention from time to time during the day, but this experience is fleeting. Recently I've become more intentional about splitting my attention. During the day I'll catch myself tuning out. As soon as I do, I'm tuned back in. I hope the more I self remember and tune in, the more this practice will become a natural way in which I operate in the world.

I encourage you to try self-remembering today. Pick an activity. It can be as simple as brushing your teeth. The next time you brush your teeth, do so paying particular attention to how you're brushing them. Are you brushing too hard? Are you reaching each tooth? Are you moving the brush up and down or sideways? At the same time tune into yourself. How are you feeling? Impatient? Or calm and relaxed? How does your body feel while you're brushing? What are you thinking? Feeling? Judgment may pop up. "I'm not doing this right." Just notice the judgment. No need to judge the judgment. Simply observe. That's consciousness, and it's the only way to plug into the divine.

Practice Four: Find the proper perspective.

I've found four tools particularly helpful in placing the ego in its proper perspective. They are:

1. Minimize the small mind;
2. Remember when;
3. Act "as if";
4. Experience "The Void."

Let's review each.

Tool One: Minimize the small mind.

When you become agitated, the ego—or small mind—has taken over. While the ego may be temporarily on the screen in your mind, know that peace—or the divine—is constantly running in the background. Then make the decision to choose peace. Visualize clicking a special key on the computer keyboard of your mind, minimizing the ego.

Try it. You'll have lots of opportunities in a given day. Let's say you're in traffic and someone cuts you off. "That jerk!" And your mind is off and running. Ah, but your observer self catches what just happened, and you don't want to go down that rabbit hole. You have chosen peace. You visualize clicking that special key on the keyboard and minimize the small mind. The ego screen disappears. In its place you see the divine. You take a deep breath and say a little mantra, "All is well."

Tool Two: Remember when.

Remember a time that you felt one with the divine? I do. I was visiting Muir Woods outside of San Francisco just after my divorce. Hiking in the beautiful giant redwood forest, I came upon a clear stream. I stopped and took a seat on the rich black earth. The sun was projecting white diamonds of light through the canopy of trees onto the forest floor. A gentle breeze brushed my cheek and the melodic sound of water flowing over moss-covered rocks filled my ears. I was totally at peace.

I read once that if during every waking hour you can remember a time that you connected with the divine for five minutes, that's better than a half day of meditation. I'm not sure about that, but this I know: I can once again experience that "peace that passes all understanding" by returning to a memory.

Tool Three: Act "as if."

We can change our circumstances by acting "as if" what we want has already happened. When we act as if, we pretend to be what we aim to become. We are no longer the seeker; we have found that which we seek. We no longer identify with the ego, but with our essence. We are perfect, whole, and divine. To do this fully we must engage the head, heart, and body. Our thoughts, our feelings, and even the way we hold our body must be involved. Let's try it. How would you hold your body differently if you were operating from your divine self? Go ahead. When I do this, I feel expanded. I sit a little taller in my seat, and my body seems to take up more space. I am more aware of the space around me—not only the space in front on me, but also the space to the sides, behind, above, and below me. And the more I concentrate on those spaces, the more they seem to expand. My body relaxes. I feel contentment, peace, and above all, love. And my thoughts? They are focused on my connection with the divine.

Tool Four: Experience "The Void."

I'm a student of the Alexander Technique, a method to relieve unwanted muscular and mental tension in the body. One of the mind-blowing things I've learned through this practice is to become more aware of the space around me. My tendency is to focus solely on what's in front of me. But when I also open up to the space behind, to the sides, below and above me, I feel such expansion. As I continue to explore this space, as I did in Tool Three, "Acting as if," I realize space is infinite. I feel the "I" of my identity fade more and more away until I feel the boundaries between my body and all that is in the world begin to blur.

When we operate totally from our divine self, we enter what Brunton calls "The Void." We are as close to God as we can possibly be while being human and alive. In The Void we are our entire being. To experience The Void is to feel like a disembodied spirit in an immense abyss of unlimited space. Perhaps this is why Brunton describes The Void as "divine darkness." Normally unobserved, we can find The Void in the infinite space between two thoughts. Here the ego vanishes, and all that remains is essence. Hence, Brunton surmises that the ego reincarnates itself with each thought.

Carrie Tiffet has written two excellent books on her personal experiences with enlightenment, *Long Time No See: Diaries of an Unlikely Messenger*, and *The Enlightenment Project*. In *The Enlightenment Project*, she offers a wonderful visualization on the void.

> *Visualize a circular cavern. It's large and clean and airy feeling. A sparkling pool of water is found at the center of the cavern. That pool of water is your Source, and it's infinitely deep. You feel good just looking at it.*
>
> *If you've brought specific worries into this cavern with you, take one last look at them and then dump that baggage by the side of the pool; there's no need to bring it beyond this point. Your Source knows what all your illusory troubles are. You're free to release them now.*
>
> *Dive into the pool. As you do so, make your body water-soluble. Feel the cells of your bones, muscles, organs and skin filling with water and gradually dissolving away until only your thinking mind and awareness remain.*
>
> *Now relax the boundaries of your thinking mind. Let its edges soften, visualizing the water as it gently fills up the thinking mind and slowly dissolves it as well.*

Now you're nothing but pure awareness. Let your awareness lose all characteristics of individuality, merging completely with that perfect water. Stay in this formless state as long as possible.

I love this meditation. I've visualized my body traveling in space. As it travels toward infinity or eternity, my body slowly diffuses until there's nothing remaining but pure consciousness.

You now have four practices that will help you still your mind and place the ego in its proper perspective. Now, here are several questions to consider.

Questions

As we discussed, the primary goal of the divine self is love. I have a new game that I'm experimenting with: I begin every day as a treasure hunt for love. All throughout the day I look for opportunities to love. As often as I can remember, I ask myself these three questions:

- Is the light of God shining through me in this moment?
- How can I bring more presence and love to this moment?
- If love is not present, what am I defending against?

This concludes our discussion on the three paths, and an excellent point for us to review several highlights of what we've learned so far. Path One concerns the evolution from the unconscious to the conscious self. Its guide is the observer self, its chief obstacle is irresponsibility, and its gift is choice. As the conscious self continues to grow, eventually it discovers the defended self. Path Two covers the evolution from the defended to the authentic self. Path Two's guide is courageous self, the chief obstacle is the status quo, and the gift is connection. As the authentic self evolves, eventually it matures into the higher self. Finally, Path Three is the path from the higher to our divine self. Holy hunger is its guide, its chief obstacle is specialness, and peace is its gift.

Remember that this is not a linear process. We often find ourselves on all three paths simultaneously, but depending on where we are in our lives, we may put more focus on one path over the other two. Above all it's important to remember that the three paths offer three strategies for how we can become more aware of who and what we are, drop the veils of illusion, and see our shining face in all of its beauty. When we are on the three paths, we are doing our work; we are doing what we were meant to do with our lives. And when we're doing the work of connecting to our selves, others, and the divine, we are preparing for a primary relationship unlike anything we could have imagined. We are ready for a spiritual partner. I believe the timing is right for three reasons:

Reason One: We are ready.

We are ready to do the work that real relationships require. Relationships offer some of the greatest classrooms around. "If life is a school, relationship is its university," writes Eva Pierrakos and Judith Saly in *Creating Union: The Essence of Intimate Relationship*. Introducing a conscious, romantic relationship into our lives is like enrolling into one of the country's top graduate schools; it challenges us to take our learning on Paths One, Two, and Three to deeper levels. In a conscious, romantic relationship we learn more about who we are, how we operate, why we do what we do, and what matters most to us. Childhood wounds surface, and we are given unprecedented opportunities to heal them. In a conscious, romantic relationship, we must become vulnerable in order to allow ourselves to be truly seen. Finally, when a relationship grows into a spiritual partnership, it becomes a vital part of our spiritual practice bringing us more in alignment with our divine selves.

Reason Two: Like attracts like.

Energy attracts similar energy. As we mentioned earlier, when we are desperate for a relationship, we are likely to attract others who are equally as desperate. When we have worked on our spiritual growth, we are likely to attract a partner who is on the same spiritual frequency as us.

Reason Three: Our intentions are clear.

As we travel the three paths, our intentions become clearer and begin to reflect our highest and best interests. Instead of seeking a primary relationship to meet some unmet need, we seek a relationship that supports and assists us in our spiritual growth. Our happiness does not depend on having such a relationship. Finding such a relationship is a preference rather than a need. One dear friend reported that finding a romantic relationship had actually lost its importance to her. "Whether I have a partner or not is of no real consequence," she shared. "Being in relationship with the divine, I am happy and at peace either way."

In her book *The Future of Love: The Power of the Soul in Intimate Relationships,* Daphne Rose Kingma writes, "This is the moment. We are being invited to move from falling in love to loving, from romance to true love, from relationships that are an undertaking of the personality to unions that are illuminated by the soul. We are being asked to mature into our true wholeness, as human beings who are in fact divine eternal souls, and we are being invited to do this *in relationship.*"

In the next section we'll examine how relationships can become a part of our spiritual practice. After reading it you may agree with me that no other spiritual path is as challenging and rewarding as being in a spiritual partnership with your romantic partner. No other path exposes our conscious and unconscious fears, doubts, insecurities, childhood wounds, and false and limiting beliefs while at the same time offering unprecedented opportunities to heal, change, and grow into our divine self and ultimately become channels of divine love.

SECTION VII

Spiritual Partnerships

The Invitation
Oriah

It doesn't interest me what you do for a living. I want to know what you ache for and if you dare to dream of meeting your heart's longing.

It doesn't interest me how old you are. I want to know if you will risk looking like a fool for love, for your dream, for the adventure of being alive.

It doesn't interest me what planets are squaring your moon. I want to know if you have touched the centre of your own sorrow, if you have been opened by life's betrayals or have become shriveled and closed from fear of further pain.

I want to know if you can sit with pain, mine or your own, without moving to hide it, or fade it, or fix it.

I want to know if you can be with joy, mine or your own; if you can dance with wildness and let the ecstasy fill you to the tips of your fingers and toes without cautioning us to be careful, be realistic, remember the limitations of being human.

It doesn't interest me if the story you are telling me is true. I want to know if you can disappoint another to be true to yourself. If you can bear the accusation of betrayal and not betray your own soul. If you can be faithless and therefore trustworthy.

I want to know if you can see Beauty even when it is not pretty every day. And if you can source your own life from its presence.

I want to know if you can live with failure, yours and mine, and still stand at the edge of the lake and shout to the silver of the full moon, 'Yes.'

It doesn't interest me to know where you live or how much money you have. I want to know if you can get up after the night of grief and despair, weary and bruised to the bone and do what needs to be done to feed the children.

It doesn't interest me who you know or how you came to be here. I want to know if you will stand in the centre of the fire with me and not shrink back.

It doesn't interest me where or what or with whom you have studied. I want to know what sustains you from the inside when all else falls away.

I want to know if you can be alone with yourself and if you truly like the company you keep in the empty moments.

A Different Kind of Relationship

I knew my relationship with Don was different when I caught myself saying to a dear friend that I had never felt so loved. I realize that this is of course because of Don. He is a lovely, loving man and I am immensely grateful to be his partner. At the same time I realize I am now in a place where I can receive and give love in a way that I've never known before. I am more open to love, and more loving as a result of my journey on these three paths. I've been delving into my unconscious and bringing what is unconscious, conscious through art, journaling, studying, therapy, and other tools and practices (Path One). I've also been working to identify and heal childhood wounds. I'm learning how to soothe that innocent, wounded inner little boy so that I can become the full expression of all I am (Path Two). Finally I'm acknowledging my inner divinity, resting in the knowledge that I am a creation of the divine and as such I am perfect as I am (Path Three). In short, I'm coming to know and love my conscious, authentic, and divine selves, and I'd like to think that I'm now operating more from those selves than from the unconscious, defended, and higher selves.

Walking these three paths brought Don into my life and helped me form a different relationship with him, the divine, and myself. I am learning that the more I love myself fully and unconditionally, the more I'm able to do so with Don. Love is like an infinity symbol that continually loops back and forth between giving and receiving love. And with each loop, our hearts open a little bit more until one day they are fully open and we are one with the divine.

I still worry that I'm unable to give the kind of full, unconditional love that I seek but recognize that this is just me being impatient. Instead of allowing shame to take over, I remember to take a deep breath and visualize love as an infinity symbol. As long as I stay on the path of giving and receiving love, my heart will continue to open and I will continue to receive and give love more fully and freely.

Life is a laboratory for love. By walking the three paths—from the unconscious to the conscious self, from the defended to the authentic self, and from the higher to the divine self—we explore the greatest gift the divine has to offer us—love, and in doing so we find what our hearts ultimately long for—unity. Not unity with "*the* One," or a romantic partner, but unity with "*The* One," the divine. And in unity with God, each other, and ourselves, our feet touch holy ground and all longing ceases.

In this section, we'll learn about spiritual partnerships. Spiritual partnerships help us learn, grow, heal, love more, and strengthen our connection to ourselves, each other, and the divine. Spiritual partners can be friends, family, or significant others—as long as there is a strong commitment to spiritual growth. Still, the most challenging and rewarding spiritual partnerships are those with romantic partners, for it's in a romantic relationship that our buttons get pushed and we learn the most. We'll discuss the people you're most likely to choose for a romantic partner and why. You'll also learn the six components of spiritual partnerships, and we'll discuss six truths about significant others as spiritual partners. You'll also learn about attracting spiritual partnerships, and we'll conclude this section with several exercises and questions.

CHAPTER FORTY-FOUR

Understand Spiritual Partnerships

At the risk of repeating myself, I want to re-emphasize that finding a romantic relationship will not relieve your longing. While some of what I'm about to reveal may be helpful in attracting a romantic partner, it will not help you find that special kind of relationship that I call a spiritual partner until you commit to consciously traveling the three paths. You have to put what's first, first.

Sometimes we can fool ourselves that we've put what's first, first when we really haven't. I did. It was not until Don and I went to visit a spiritual healer in South America that something shifted for me, and I turned my primary focus to Path Three. I still can't wrap words around my experience, but I can tell you this: I'm still on Paths One and Two, but Path Three has become my central focus. Nothing is more important than my connection with the divine and my divine self. Not even Don.

When we experience our divine selves, we also experience divine love. It's only then that we have some inkling of the potential of a relationship that encompasses such a love. We begin to realize that having just a romantic relationship is not enough, we want something even better: a romantic relationship that is a spiritual partnership.

According to Gary Zukav, spiritual partnership is a relationship between equals for the purpose of spiritual growth. In his book *Beyond Religion,* David Elkins writes that's it's "a spiritual training ground, a place where we slowly give up self-centeredness and learn the meaning of patience, forgiveness, compassion, and love." He says it's not so much a two-way street as it is a triangle where the sacred sits at the apex.

We enter spiritual partnerships to learn, grow, heal, love more, and strengthen our connection to our selves, all of creation, and divinity. I like to think of spiritual partnerships as a kind of graduate program for the soul, and the three paths as our curriculum. Let's take a brief look at that curriculum.

Path One: The Evolution from the Unconscious to the Conscious Self

Path One teaches us how to become fully active participants rather than emotionally unconscious sleepwalkers. On Path One we can learn things about ourselves in a spiritual relationship that we could never learn anywhere else, since the quality of our relationship with a partner mirrors the quality of our relationship to ourselves. We learned earlier that much about ourselves remains unconscious, and much of what is unconscious is projected. Then it stands to reason that one of the best means of bringing what is unconscious, conscious are relationships—especially those we describe as spiritual relationships whose sole purpose is for growth.

Path Two: The Evolution from the Defended to the Authentic Self

Path Two helps us do the emotional homework necessary to clear away many of the defenses that prevent us from loving fully, including our core wounds and false beliefs. And spiritual partnership is the perfect place for us to practice vulnerability and authenticity because we feel safe in them.

Path Three: The Evolution from the Higher to the Divine Self

Path Three shows us how to return home to the state of spiritual consciousness that is pure or divine love. If love is the most direct way to essence, then spiritual partnership is the highway to the divine. Spiritual partnership allows us to explore forgiveness, acceptance, support, and unconditional love. By learning to love our partner, despite his or her humanness and flaws, we learn to love ourselves and acknowledge our own divinity.

Since spiritual partnership strives to operate from the divine self rather than the ego, it is built on love—not fear. When we base our intentions, communications, decisions, and actions on love, we minimize the need for clinging, judging, jealousy, competition, and other ego-based insecurities. Instead of trying to change our partner, we seek to learn more about ourselves and deepen our connection to our selves, all of creation, and God. We do our best to love our partner unconditionally, doing all in our power to create a safe place where each partner feels seen, heard, understood, appreciated, and above all, loved.

A spiritual partnership is not the same as a soul mate. Traditional lore would have you believe that once you find your soul mate, you are complete. Picture two half circles that form a whole. A spiritual partnership is different; envision two complete circles that overlap, like a Venn diagram. There are three separate entities: you, your partner, and a third, the relationship. Each circle is complete, whole, perfect, and divine, but they are linked together to form an even stronger union. A spiritual partnership places "I" in the context of "We," without losing the "I" and becoming codependent. We take responsibility for our lives and happiness—our thoughts, feelings and actions. We constantly remind ourselves, "This is not about my partner—this is about me." And our partners do the same.

While it's important to honor and assist the other on his or her spiritual journey, it's equally important not to take responsibility for it. Respect implies equality. We have to trust our partner to find his or her own answers. This means refraining from judging, interpreting, analyzing, and comparing our spiritual journey to his or hers. In a spiritual partnership, each partner has his or her own relationship with the divine, but he has consciously committed to making the relationship an integral part of his spiritual practice. Every aspect of the relationship as well as every circumstance—both good and bad—serves to bring each partner closer to themselves, all of creation, and God.

"I" in the Context of "We"

Spiritual partners keep us honest, and we are better people for having them in our lives. My friend Ginny is that way. When I'm complaining about something Don has or hasn't done, she reminds me to not be so self-serving: "Randy, you just don't like to be inconvenienced." In a gentle way—well maybe not *that* gentle—Ginny calls me out when I'm being selfish, stubborn, unaware, or disrespectful of Don's perspective.

Spiritual partners see the best in us—sometimes before we can see it for ourselves. My friend Ruth did this for me. Some years ago she told me that it wasn't my accomplishments that attracted her to me—it was my big heart. "My big heart?" I exclaimed. She must be thinking of someone else. Being someone who spends a great deal of time in his head, I didn't consider myself much of a feeler, much less someone with a big heart. Regardless, Ruth was patient and persistent. She held the belief that I was big hearted until I could claim it for myself.

Romantic Spiritual Partnerships

While spiritual partners can be friends or family, the unions that provide the greatest growth opportunities are those with a romantic partner. In fact, I can think of no faster way toward psychological and spiritual wholeness, in part because romantic spiritual partnerships provide the biggest mirrors. When we talk about mirrors and relationships, we are referring to the process of projection. We've already talked a good bit about how we project shadow attributes—both positive and negative—onto others. Nowhere do we do this more than with our partners. For example, every serious relationship I've had since my divorce has been with a man whom I would call gentle. Looking into the mirror of projection, it's clear that I've not yet fully integrated my own gentleness.

Another reason romantic spiritual partnerships offer the greatest growth potential is that they also offer the greatest opportunity for psychological and spiritual healing. Harville Hendrix, Ph.D. and his wife Helen LeKelly Hunt have authored many books, including *Getting The Love You Want: A Guide for Couples*. They are also the creators of Imago Relationship Therapy, which teaches that we are attracted to those who have the capacity to wound us in similar ways that we felt wounded by our parents. Why? To finish the unfinished business of childhood, heal, and return to wholeness. Imago Relationship Therapy seeks to align the conscious mind (that typically is focused on feeling good) with the unconscious mind (that is focused on of the goal of healing and growth). Hendrix explains that we choose partners for two reasons: the first is that they have the positive and negative traits of the people who raised us; and second, our partners compensate for positive parts of our being that we sent to the basement of our shadow in childhood. For example, a man who had a smothering mother may only be attracted to strong, domineering women. A woman who had a father who was overly protective may then seek out a man who will continue to protect her. We seem to have a natural ability to select partners who share traits similar to the parent who wounded us most.

Hendrix writes, "Our unconscious drive to repair the emotional damage of childhood is what allows us to realize our spiritual potential as human beings, to become complete and loving people capable of nurturing others." If you subscribe to these basic tenets of Imago Relationship Therapy, as I do, then you will conclude that the greatest opportunities for spiritual growth come not only with a partner with whom we share a safe, intimate relationship, but also with what Hendrix and Hunt call an "Imago match," someone so similar to our caregivers that our unconscious mind has them fused. I invite you to take a minute to reflect—or even better, journal—about how this could be true for you.

In this chapter, we defined spiritual partnerships and discussed how we choose partners on this journey. Next we'll explore the first of six components of a spiritual partnership. According to Gary Zukav, spiritual partnerships have four main components:

- Commitment
- Courage
- Compassion
- Conscious Communication

While I agree with Zukav's list, I would add two additional components: curiosity and confrontation. Curiosity is what keeps Eros alive, and Eros is critical to healthy and happy relationships. Confrontation—along with compassion—keeps us honest and on a spiritual track.

CHAPTER FORTY-FIVE

Commitment

I believe it's important to make three commitments in a spiritual partnership: one to the relationship, another to what we've agreed upon, and a final one to staying emotionally present. Love is not enough. In order for a relationship to survive, there must also be commitment. Commitment means we act with integrity, respect, and compassion—even when we might feel differently. Love will not help us weather the storm, but commitment will. I recently read about a survey where 85 percent of divorced couples indicated a "lack of commitment to the marriage and to each other" as their reason for divorce. Commitment to the relationship is critical if each partner is going to feel safe in the relationship, but it is not a guarantee. Commitment is only a statement of intent. Commitments also are a choice, and they are a choice to make moment to moment in a spiritual partnership.

Several years after moving to Asheville, I attended a workshop given by Maureen McCarthy and Zelle Nelson, a married couple who co-created something called "The Blueprint of We," formerly called "the State of Grace Document." Maureen and Zelle describe "The Blueprint of We" as a collaborative process used to build and sustain healthier, more resilient business and personal relationships. I see it as an excellent tool for creating intentional and committed relationships. It is made up of five components:

1. The Story of Us: a narrative of how the two parties came together and how they see each other while things are going smoothly.
2. Interaction styles and warning signs: a summary of how each party likes to be communicated with and what might trigger each partner. For example, in my relationship with Don, I might get short or snappy if I'm hungry or over-tired. I also warn him that when I return home from being out of town for a while, I need to be alone for several hours while I unpack, attend to mail, and answer emails.

3. Expectations: an overview of the type of relationship each party is seeking. For example, it's important to both Don and me that our relationship be monogamous.

4. Questions for peace and prosperity: a list of questions everyone agrees to answer if the relationship goes awry. These questions are designed to bring the partners back in harmony. They could include: "What am I afraid of?," "What truth do I need to tell?," and "What do I need most from you right now?"

5. Long and short term agreements: these specify when the parties will meet should they run into rough water. Don and I have an agreement not to go to bed angry with the other, and should the unimaginable happen and we break up, we agree to sit down and talk within one year after we separate.

Whether formal or informal, commitments should be reviewed, renegotiated, and renewed periodically to keep them fresh and alive. A friend and his wife "contract" to be in relationship from one year to the next. As part of their contract to one another, at least once a year they sit down and review the wedding vows they wrote for one another. Commitment also entails taking responsibility for our role in creating a healthy relationship. Zukav suggests that it's particularly important to stay attuned to our reactions, emotions, and intentions. I believe it's also imperative to try to be as transparent as possible.

We want to be constantly learning about ourselves by examining our thoughts, emotions, intentions, and reactions—such as anger, fear, jealousy, resentment, and impatience. We also want to be hyper-aware of what reactions belong to us, our partner, and to the relationship, rather than simply cast blame on our partner when things get off balance. A while back, *O Magazine* featured an article by Dr. David Burns, associate professor of psychology at Stanford University School of Medicine, which studied long-term satisfaction in intimate relationships. Fifteen hundred people responded, and their results reflected their belief that only one thing had a causal impact on the success or failure of these relationships: not blaming your partner for problems that come up.

Being committed to a spiritual partnership means much more than simply staying in the relationship—it also means that you be emotionally present. Zen master Thich Nhat Hanh writes, "When you love someone, the best thing you can offer is your presence. How can you love if you are not there?" I've found it's far easier to stay emotionally present when things are going well than when they get tough.

When Don and I first moved in together, we started seeing a couple's therapist. When she asked our goals, one of mine was to stay present in the relationship. "I don't want Don to become like the wallpaper," I explained. Staying emotionally present in the relationship continues to be a challenge for me. It's sometimes difficult for me to identify what I'm feeling, and it's even harder for me to talk about it. This is why the next component—courage—has been so important to me. I'm finding the courage to share my thoughts and feelings despite any fears around being abandoned when I speak my truth.

CHAPTER FORTY-SIX

Courage

The defended self is the driver of most unconscious relationships. In order to defend our image and guard against being hurt, we armor our most authentic selves. A spiritual partnership operates from an entirely different tactic. It finds the courage to self-reveal, expose the raw edges, be vulnerable, and show its most tender and tentative self.

"Okay, I hear you," a friend said after I shared my thoughts around self-revelation and relationship, "but a lot of times I don't know how I feel or what I'm experiencing." "Then share that!" I replied. "What's important is to keep the lines of communication open. Speak your truth as you know it."

Most of us have it wrong. Showing our true nature doesn't make us weaker, and our partners don't love us less for our imperfection. We are stronger and more lovable when we find the courage to share our most authentic selves. Finding the courage to self-reveal is one of the most important components of a spiritual partnership. Without it, it's impossible for us to fulfill one of our greatest desires: to feel seen, heard, understood, and loved for all we are. It should be pretty evident by now that to be in a spiritual partnership requires that we be both vulnerable and transparent, holding nothing back. Daphne Kingma writes, "Each time we tell a truth we become more transparent, more visible, more at the mercy of one another's love."

I read once that when it comes to expressing truth and vulnerability, most people favor one over the other. This is certainly true for me. I can be vulnerable, but to speak my truth can feel like a herculean task. Even speaking the most simple and benign truth, even a compliment rather than a complaint, feels like conflict. It also feels like a threat. Deep down I'm afraid that if I speak my truth, my partner will leave me. If I'm truly committed to a spiritual partnership, I have to find the courage to speak out, regardless of my fears, for it's what we don't say in a relationship that kills it. Withholding any information—even positive and seemingly inconsequential information such as appreciations and compliments—erodes relationships over time.

Recently a friend shared a wonderful article from a blog, ReidAboutSext.com, in which the author, Reid Mihalko, describes a terrific two-step formula to craft a difficult conversation.

Step One: Reid advises answering these questions for three to five minutes without lifting the pen or pausing keystrokes. Just get the "crap on paper" he counsels.

Question A: "What I'm not saying to my partner is _____.

Question B: What I'm afraid might happen if I say it is _____.

Question C: What I'd like to happen by saying this is _____.

Step Two: Organize the conversation by cutting and pasting your answers into this script:

Dear _____.

There are some things I've not been saying to you. I'm not saying them/haven't been able to say them because I'm afraid the following might happen. *(Insert answers from Question B here.)*

What I would like to have happen by my telling you is: *(Insert answers from Question C here.)*

Thank you for listening. What, if anything, do you want to share?

I tried it with Don and my conversation went something like this:

There is something that I've not said to you that I'd like to. I haven't said it before because I've been scared that you might leave me if I do.

I'd like you to just listen. There's nothing to fix here. Only hear me out. Is that okay with you?

I've been struggling at times with how to balance being with you, which I love, and getting enough time to myself. I worry at times that you don't have more outside interests, and then I catch myself and realize that you are not me. You might not need a lot of outside activity. And that if I am feeling smothered in any way, that is my stuff, not yours. I simply need to figure out what I need and share it with you.

Thank you for listening. Okay, is there anything you want to ask or say?

It wasn't as hard as I thought it would be. It's okay if you want to print out your script and read it. I did. Do whatever makes you more comfortable, but share it with your partner. It's worth it. Believe me.

Vulnerability engenders intimacy, authenticity, and being in the present moment. Brené Brown writes in *Daring Greatly*, "Vulnerability is the birthplace of love, belonging, joy, courage, empathy, and creativity. It is the source of hope, empathy, accountability, and authenticity. If we want greater clarity in our purpose, or deeper and more meaningful spiritual lives, vulnerability is the path." Vulnerability takes great courage and is well worth the risk.

CHAPTER FORTY-SEVEN

Compassion

The third component of a spiritual partnership is compassion. The word "compassion" comes from the Latin word "patior" and the Greek work "pathein," meaning to suffer, undergo, or experience. To be compassionate means that we experience something with another person—or to borrow an old expression, "We walk a mile in their shoes." When we are compassionate, we immerse ourselves in another's viewpoint, feel their pain or happiness as if it were our own, and keep our focus on the other person without getting swept away by emotions—theirs or ours.

Compassion for both our partners and ourselves is a critical component of a spiritual partnership. Practicing self-compassion not only makes individuals healthier and happier, it is also a good predictor of healthy romantic relationships, according to a study by University of Texas at Austin educational psychologists Kristin Neff and Tasha Beretvas. This should come as little surprise—we cannot give to others what we don't have ourselves.

I used to berate myself for not being more affectionate with my partner. Beating up on myself did nothing but make me feel inadequate, which wasn't good for me or the relationship. Then I realized the source of my discomfort: we rarely showed affection in our family, and if you did you could be subject to ridicule. Once I connected these dots, I was able to be more compassionate with myself. Showing affection still doesn't come as naturally as I would like, but I'm becoming more comfortable with it.

Research shows that spouses who love each other compassionately stay together longer, are happier, and support one another more effectively than couples who do not love each other compassionately. This should come as no surprise. Being compassionate doesn't require fixing problems or agreeing with your partner. It calls only for giving him or her our full attention and presence. Compassionate love recognizes the partner's specific positive and negative qualities while simultaneously affirming the partner's overall worth. From time to time, the frightened parts of our personalities will show. When this happens we can shift things and react from a place of love by remembering innocence—ours and our partner's.

At times, it helps me to visualize Don as a little boy. On the bookshelf behind my desk sits a small stuffed elephant that belonged to Don when he was a child. Don loved this toy very much. It's missing an eye and its soft grey coat is stained. Every time I see it, I'm reminded of Don's sweetness and innocence. Don's battered childhood elephant helps me remember that when Don becomes frustrated or angry with me, it's often the frightened "little boy" who is reacting. I'm able then to respond more with compassion, patience, and love. Marianne Williamson offers another suggestion for finding compassion for our mates in her book *Return to Love*. She suggests this simple prayer: "Dear God, I surrender this relationship to you. Let me see this person through your eyes."

CHAPTER FORTY-EIGHT

Conscious Communication

Conscious communication is on Zukav's list of guidelines for spiritual partnerships. He writes that successful conscious communication requires:
- Consulting our intuition;
- Speaking personally and specifically (using "I" statements rather than "we" or "you" statements);
- Releasing attachment to outcomes and trusting in the Universe;
- Choosing intentions before speaking or acting;
- Acting from the healthiest part of our personalities.

While I agree with all of these, there's another requirement that's equally important: creating a "safe container." Communication is the centerpiece of all connection. Dr. Sue Johnson, author of *Hold Me Tight: Seven Conversations for a Lifetime of Love*, offers these wise words about connection, "Until we address the fundamental need for connection and the fear of losing it, the standard techniques, such as learning problem-solving or communications skills, examining childhood hurts, or taking time-outs, are misguided and ineffectual." In other words, despite what many of the relationship experts are telling us, there's nothing more important to a relationship—and communication in that relationship—than creating what I call "a safe container." Without one, all the other strategies for keeping a relationship alive and healthy are moot.

When we create a safe container, we create a space that welcomes all parts of a person, known and unknown, comfortable and uncomfortable, spoken and unspoken. You and your partner have created this space in which you can talk to him or her about literally anything—without fear of judgment, criticism, or repercussion. Creating a safe container is critical if we're striving to meet the goal of conscious communication: to tell our truth and to hear our partner's truth. To do this, we have to substitute responsibility for blame, and listen without judgment. This can be especially hard when we are in pain.

Pain is a wake-up call. In a spiritual relationship, when we discover we are in pain it's time to pause and see what's going on. This begins with what we're feeling. Am I feeling sad, angry, resentful, or jealous? Once I identify the emotions, I can explore the cause, and the cause is often an unmet need. This is where I get into trouble—it's too easy to blame my partner for not meeting my need, and then try to shame him into feeling guilty.

Sometimes I haven't even shared with my partner that I'm upset, much less why. But in order to create and protect our safe container, I must find the courage to share what I'm feeling, without blame, and take full responsibility for my feelings. When I do this, I almost always feel better, and inevitably we become closer as a couple. I say something like this: "When you drove up and saw me in the yard working and did not offer to help, I found myself martyring out. Then I got resentful and angry. I'm pretty sure it triggered some old childhood wounds of not feeling supported." In sharing my truth, I'm not asking Don to apologize or even pitch in—only bear witness to my feelings. When the situation is reversed and Don shares something painful with me, I want to learn to say to myself something like this, "This is Don's experience. What I think or feel about it is not as important as it is to listen closely and try to understand it." Unfortunately this is especially hard for Don and me. As former consultants, we are hardwired to be fixers. We have to remind ourselves, "I don't have to do anything and I don't have to fix anything. My job is only to listen and understand." Once I've done that, then I can ask Don what he needs from me.

This is a process, and I'm still learning and evolving. I've taken numerous workshops and read so many books that offer pat formulas on how to structure communication, but unfortunately few have helped. In the stress of the moment I might forget the right wording or get the sequence out of order. But I've found that if I listen to Don with the intent of truly understanding his experience, and speak my own truth without blame, while taking full responsibility for my thoughts, feelings, and actions, I'm able to blunder through it. Then both of us end up feeling heard.

CHAPTER FORTY-NINE

Curiosity

When we are in relationship with a romantic partner, there are three elements at play, each of which correlates to one of our three centers of intelligence. The first is love—love corresponds to the heart center of intelligence. Then there's Eros, which is associated with the head, and finally we have sex, which is connected to the gut.

Sanskrit has ninety-six different words for love, ancient Persia had eighty, Greece three, and in the West we have one. There are so many ways to look at and define love. For example, to love your meal is quite different than loving your boyfriend. For the purpose of our conversation though, we'll use this simple definition of love: "to feel a deep romantic attachment to someone." We'll define Eros as mental, physical, emotional, sexual, and spiritual attraction. John O'Donohue in *Beauty* defines Eros: "Eros is a divine force. It infuses all the earth. Yet, too often, in our culture Eros is equated with lust and sexual greed. But it is a more profound and sacred force than this. Eros is the light of wisdom that awakens and guides the sensuous." Finally, there's sex. Again, we'll go with a simple definition: "Sexual activity, including specifically, sexual intercourse."

In romantic relationships we tend to put all the emphasis on love and sex, forgetting what I've come to believe is the lifeblood of all healthy relationship: Eros. Eros is the critical piece of the puzzle that often determines if a relationship succeeds or fails over the long haul. Eros is present when we feel we have new things to learn about our partner, and it's present when we are willing to reveal more about ourselves.

On the contrary, it's when we think we know all there is to know about our loved one that the relationship begins to wither. I was the worst at making assumptions. I assumed I knew what Don was thinking or feeling and I also assumed that he knew what I was thinking—or worse didn't care. Like most couples, we spent a lot of time together in silence. That's fine when both parties are seeking silence, but it's not so fine when it's because we assume we have nothing to say to one another. Those periods of awkward silence with Don occur less frequently since I've started sharing what I'm thinking, even when I think my thoughts are trivial and insignificant. If nothing else, we can laugh at how random or non-secular my thoughts can be. I've also stopped assuming I know anything about what Don is feeling or thinking. Instead, I ask him, and I'm finding myself surprised at how often I think he's upset about something when he's not.

At the same time, we have to be willing to be seen and known by our partners. Brené Brown writes in her book *Daring Greatly*, "We cultivate love when we allow our most vulnerable and powerful selves to be deeply seen and known, and when we honor the spiritual connection that grows from that offering with trust, respect, kindness, and affection." I record my dreams, insights, fears, and most intimate thoughts in my journal. I write for my eyes only, and yet every time I share an entry with Don, it brings us closer.

Eros stimulates deep sharing and contributes to deeper connection in relationships. It also feeds us spiritually. "In a spiritually highly developed person, the erotic force carries the entity from the erotic experience, which in itself is of short duration, into the permanent state of pure love," Eva Pierrakos and Judith Saly teach in *Creating Union: The Essence of Intimate Relationship*. They continue, "Eros gives the soul a foretaste of unity and teaches the fearful psyche the longing for it. The more strongly one has experienced Eros, the less contentment will the soul find in the pseudo-security of separateness."

CHAPTER FIFTY

Confrontation

Confrontation is the sixth and final component of spiritual partnerships. It's important in a number of ways. First, confrontation holds each person accountable for being his or her best. Second, when issues arise—as they do with all couples—it's important to feel free to air them. And finally, as we saw earlier, the more we learn about our partner's thoughts and feeling, the more intimacy we share.

As I mentioned earlier, my friend Ginny and I are spiritual partners. A while back we made a pact: we would be each other's comforters *and* confronters. We would be empathetic while at the same time not pull any punches when the other is deceiving him or herself. Truth-telling takes courage, and it's more likely to be received if it's done with compassion. The other day I was complaining about something trivial that Don had done, and Ginny reminded me of how happy I've been since Don moved in. She would know; Ginny has been my confidant through every relationship since my divorce. Her gentle nudging immediately shifted my perspective from irritation to gratitude.

Don and I often nudge each other to his best or higher self. For example, Don and I both grew up with parents who were affected by the Great Depression. To save money, my mother used to save tin foil. Don's mother was likewise a master in stretching a dollar. As a result we both can be chintzy, operating from a sense of lack rather than abundance. In a non-shaming way we often remind each other of the importance of being freer with our money, especially with those who have less than we do.

In a spiritual partnership, confrontation is even more important because we are more likely to trigger each other's defense mechanisms. Intentionally or not, we are going to rattle each other's cages. When we do, defenses go up and we can lose track of our highest and divine selves. When our partners confront us with compassion, we can find our way back.

Some couples love to fight; others don't. Don and I are one of those couples who hate confrontation. If we remain unconscious and on autopilot, we can let things pile up until they blow. I know better. I know that every time we've had a disagreement, we've come out of it just fine. In fact our relationship grew stronger. Finding the courage to both give and receive feedback provides great opportunities for growth.

What makes disagreements particularly challenging for most couples is that they tend to focus on trivial matters without taking time to uncover the central issue. For example, arguments around sex often are about intimacy. Or a disagreement concerning money may be more about power. In addition to identifying the central issue, it's also critical to show respect for our partner and his or her opinions—even in the heat of an argument.

As I've mentioned, Don and I are renovating a vacation house at the beach. In this process we've faced hundreds of decisions together, and in most cases we've agreed on how to resolve them. On the rare occasions we do disagree and end up in a fight, it's because I've dismissed Don's opinion or preference without having considered his point of view. Don's reaction has been to get angry—and rightly so—because I haven't shown respect. It's not because I have a different opinion or preference. I've found that the most important thing is that each person feels heard, seen, and understood. We may not agree, but we feel validated and heard—and that's what really matters in the end. The same issue will probably come up again and again down the road, but as long as each partner feels heard, it will be okay. There's wisdom in the old maxim: "We agree to disagree."

The problem comes when we make disagreements into a win-lose proposition. Disagreements are about communication, not competition. The only way to lose is to not listen with an open heart. I have a friend who has been in a happy relationship for over thirty years, and I asked him what he felt was the most important ingredient in their relationship. Without hesitation he replied, "Listening. I've learned it's much better to understand before trying to be understood."

While fighting can strengthen a relationship, it's important to pick your battles. Not every issue has to be discussed and resolved. John Gottman has been called the Michael Jordan of relationship research. The author of nine books, Gottman counsels that couples don't need to communicate and resolve all of their problems. In his research of thousands of happily married couples, some of whom have been married for over forty years, he found that most successful couples have persistent unresolved issues, some of which they've been fighting about for decades. Successful couples accept and understand that some conflict is inevitable, and that there always will be certain things they don't like about their partner or a subject in which they don't agree. He concludes that we shouldn't feel the need to change our partner in order to love him or her, nor should we allow some disagreements to get in the way of what is otherwise a great relationship. The bottom-line? Sometimes the most optimal relationship strategy is "live and let live."

I want to support Don's spiritual growth, and at times that's going to mean confronting Don. But above all, I have to remember that Don has his own path, and that path is different than mine. I am not his life coach, teacher, therapist, personal trainer, spiritual guide, or father. My primary job is to love, accept, encourage, and support—not monitor, nag, judge, or demand. I am here to support Don in being his best, and most of the time that's best accomplished by listening and being the best person I can be.

CHAPTER FIFTY-ONE

Six Truths about Spiritual Partners

Earlier we talked about the myths around about spiritual partners as significant others. Now I'd like to discuss six truths. Much of this comes from the work of one of my favorite writers, Paul Ferrini.

Truth One: Spiritual partnerships take hard work.

A student once asked Ram Dass about relationships. At first Dass responded with a superficial answer, but when the student persisted he said, "Well, if you really want to look at love from the spiritual side, you can make relationship your yoga, but it is the hardest yoga you'll ever do."

When we don't do the work, we simply change actors—but the roles and sets remain the same. It's not until we work hard on rewriting the script that our relationships can change for better. But the work doesn't stop there. In his book *Still Life with Woodpecker,* Tom Robbins writes: "When two people meet and fall in love, there's a sudden rush of magic. Magic is just naturally present then. We tend to feed on that gratuitous magic without striving to make any more. One day we wake up and find that the magic is gone. We hustle to get it back, but by then it's usually too late, we've used it up. What we have to do is work like hell at making additional magic right from the start. It's hard work, but if we can remember to do it, we greatly improve our chances of making love stay."

Truth Two: The tough times are the richest.

It's during the tough times that relationships have the capacity to strengthen, and we have the opportunity to grow. In his book *I Am the Door,* Paul Ferrini reminds us, "Relationship is like a giant backhoe. It digs down through the superficial layers of consciousness and exposes your deepest fears and insecurities. …There is perhaps no more rapid path to psychological wholeness and spiritual awakening than the path of relationship."

Tough times awaken us from the daily routines of life and relationships and breaths new life into a relationship. When approached with openness and truth, they help us see each other more clearly and they bring us closer together. What sustains us through rough patches is the knowledge that we're together for the larger purpose of supporting each other's spiritual growth and that the greatest growth takes place during difficult times. In short, the more we mine these tough times, the more we grow capacities to love.

Truth Three: Loving someone is a choice—not a feeling—and it's a choice that we make moment to moment.

Falling in love is no more than infatuation, and infatuation passes. The feeling we call love isn't consistent—it waxes and wanes. Solid relationships require consistency. Like fine wine, rich relationships mature over time, but unlike a fine wine they must be attended to constantly. From moment to moment we must choose love. Spiritual guide Shirley Stinard dislikes the word "relationship." She likes to say, "There's either love or no-love." In every instant we have a choice to act out of love, or not—and each choice ultimately determines the quality of our relationship.

Jim and Beth have been together for six years. Jim is basically a kind man, but there's little passion in their relationship. They share few common interests, and sex is infrequent. Jim has never cheated on Beth. Earlier in life, Jim was an athlete, but he has gotten sedentary and soft around the middle. Beth wonders if she's settling. Should she consider leaving? It's a common story that many of us experience in long-term relationships. What once seemed extraordinary has become ordinary—if not dull, and the relationship has become a source of anger, frustration, and disappointment. One option is to bail. Another is to re-engage and choose love.

Instead of focusing on our partner's shortcomings or our wants and needs, we can shift our focus to the relationship itself. We can make love our primary relationship and see our partner as an opportunity to give love independent of what he or she is doing or not doing for us. When we choose love as our primary relationship, we find the contentment, meaning, and happiness that we've been seeking.

Truth Four: Spiritual partners banish the scorekeeper.

Unlike most relationships, spiritual partners focus on what they are putting into a relationship rather than what they are getting out of them. We choose to love with no expectation of anything in return. Love is freely given for the pure joy of it—no strings. When we begin to keep score, we catch ourselves knowing that the ego has taken control.

I love planning and preparing meals for Don, but every now and then I find myself becoming resentful. When this happens I know the scorekeeper has taken over. Don does more than his share around the house, but this seldom satisfies the scorekeeper. The scorekeeper thrives on being a martyr. Thankfully Don and I now find humor in this, and when the scorekeeper starts martyring out, we can laugh about it. Then Don pitches in, and we cook dinner together.

Truth Five: Spiritual partners strive to operate from essence or their divine selves.

The divine self has one overriding goal: to love fully. When we operate from essence, love is transformed. Kingma writes in her book *The Future of Love*, "The highest level of this transformation, which may take decades and many partners to achieve, or may never be fulfilled in a single lifetime, is reached when we are able simply to embrace another person with nothing but the grace of pure love, with total perception, total reception, total acceptance. The ultimate goal of all relationship experiences is to deliver us to this place of pure love—no judgment, no ax to grind, no needs to whimper over or insist on being fulfilled. Just love, Pure love."

We learn to love our partners' imperfections and in doing so accept the imperfection in ourselves. American author, professor and philosopher Sam Keen once wrote, "You come to love not by finding the perfect person, but by seeing an imperfect person perfectly." Keen's quote reminds me of a friend who is an artist with a mental disability. His mother was his primary caregiver, and she was a collector—she collected imperfect things. For example, she had a pot that wasn't quite centered and a doll with arms that didn't quite match. She found beauty in each imperfect object. Wabi-sabi is a Japanese art of finding beauty in imperfection. In her book *Wabi Sabi Love: The Ancient Art of Finding the Perfect Love in Imperfect Relationships,* Arielle Ford applies the concept of wabi-sabi to relationships, writing that wabi-sabi love is the art and practice of appreciating the irritations, quirks, limitations, and imperfections in our partners and in ourselves. She explains, "I believe a big part of this problem is that the media and society have brainwashed us and conditioned us to look for and see perfection, which leads to an ongoing state of frustration and dissatisfaction. In truth, we all know that perfection is not possible. I believe the word perfection needs to be changed to 'Pure Fiction!' So giving up perfection and embracing imperfection is the way to go."

When we are operating from our defended self, we tend to focus on what our partners are missing rather than all the wonderful things our partner brings to our life. Stronger relationships hone in on what's good in the relationship—the bigger picture—instead of what is missing. Instead of trying to change our partners, we need to change our perceptions. "First, you must be willing to make a shift in your perception and see your current situation and your mate's behavior through a new, gentler, and kinder lens. Chances are you see their behavior as 'wrong or bad.' But, imagine for a moment that this behavior exists solely to teach you how to become a more loving, compassionate person. Can you find the gift of that behavior?" Ford asks.

In *Wabi Sabi Love,* Ford tells the story of Ed and Deb. Ed loves to meet new people and tell silly jokes. Deb had heard all of these jokes a million times and is often annoyed because she feels she's always waiting for him while he's entertaining strangers. One day after Deb had waited for Ed for the third time in less than an hour, she watched Ed befriending a little boy sitting on the curb waiting for his mother. She heard Ed ask the boy, "How does a camel hide in the desert?" The boy gave him a puzzled look, and then Ed delivered the punch line: "Camelflage." With that the boy burst out laughing. It was at that moment that Deb finally got Ed's true nature. He wasn't trying to make her crazy. He just loved making people happy. Deb found the beauty and perfection in what once made her crazy. Deb found wabi-sabi love.

I think to myself, well good for Deb, but she doesn't have to deal with Don's.... Then I catch myself. Once again I'm being critical about something Don has or hasn't done. I don't want to be that person, and I don't want us to be that couple. You know what I'm talking about: that couple that is always criticizing one another publically. More often than not I do the same thing I'm criticizing Don for. By loving Don's imperfections and forgiving him any transgressions, I love and forgive my own. I read once that we can only be as happy with another person as we are with ourselves. Only when we know, accept, and love ourselves, can we know, accept, and love another.

I keep in mind that just as we all have gifts, we all have areas that are less developed. It's easy to judge Don on those areas in which I might be more skilled than he, and to forget that Don also has areas in which he is the expert. For example, Don is much more mechanical than me—he can fix most anything. He also is far more patient than I am. By focusing on the positive instead of the negative, I'll be much happier, and our relationship will become healthier.

Truth Six: Sometimes we outgrow relationships— even spiritual partnerships.

I believe that every relationship has a beginning, a middle, and an end. The end may come with a death of a partner, or when we've learned what we came together to learn. And sometimes we outgrow partners, or they outgrow us. When this happens, we separate with as much love as we can muster, accepting the end as the natural cycle of things and remembering there's no need for shame. Relationships are spiritual assignments.

Sometimes it's easy to know it's time to move on. For example, you're in an abusive relationship and you've had enough. Other times it's not so easy. Perhaps your partner cheats on you. Some of the relationships that I admire most have withstood some pretty rough bumps in the road. Yet the couples persevered and now enjoy a stronger, deeper connection.

I remember breaking up with a woman I was dating in college because she wasn't spiritual enough. Her response still haunts me: "You never gave me a chance." She was right. I acted on assumptions rather than trying to find the courage to talk with her about my fears. I've often wondered if I've given up too soon on relationships in the past. Perhaps I have. Then I remember that I wouldn't have Don now had I not.

I have no illusions. If relationships take work, then spiritual partnerships take even more work. Great relationships require enormous efforts towards consciousness, consistency, and courage, but I also know the rewards are well worth the effort. I also know that at times I'll be triggered and I'll jump back into my defended self. That's a part of being human. All of us have our blind spots, hidden agendas, fears, insecurities, emotional trigger points, and manipulative tendencies, and the chances are pretty good that they're going to show up from time to time. I am imperfect, Don is imperfect, and our love—well, it's going to be imperfect too. To expect anything else is only setting the stage for disappointment. Will Don and I be in a "forever relationship?" I have no way of knowing, but I certainly hope so. If not, I hope we'll find the courage to leave the relationship with as much love, honesty, and grace as we began it.

CHAPTER FIFTY-TWO

Attract a Spiritual Partner

I believe that when we are on the three paths, a spiritual partnership will come to us. We don't have to go looking for it. That doesn't absolve us of all responsibility, however. In her book *Enchanted Love,* Marianne Williamson writes: "When love isn't in our lives, it's on the way. If you know that a special guest is coming at five o'clock, do you spend the day messing up the home? Of course not. You prepare. And that is what we should do for love." And how do we prepare? By doing our inner work.

I've read a plethora of books on how to find a romantic partner, and the better ones concentrate on the inner rather than the outer world. First, we have far more control of our inner life than the outer one. Second, when we prepare our inner life we are in a far stronger position to attract what we seek in the outer world. For example, until we're able to find peace and contentment alone, we'll never be able to experience it in a relationship.

I know of no better way to prepare for a spiritual partner than Paths One, Two, and Three. When we bring what is unconscious to consciousness, soothe our defended self so that we can become a fuller expression of all we are, and evolve from our highest to our divine selves, we are doing the work that we came here to do. We are more centered and at peace, and as such more likely to attract a spiritual partner to assist in taking this work deeper.

Pragmatically, we can prepare for partnership by examining our fantasies, myths, projections, and limiting beliefs around relationships. We can also study past relationships to determine whom we've been attracting and why. There's a wonderful poem by Portia Nelson that illustrates the wisdom of examining past patterns.

Autobiography in Five Short Chapters
Portia Nelson

Chapter 1
I walk down the street.
There is a deep hole in the sidewalk.
I fall in.
I am lost ... I am helpless.
It isn't my fault.
It takes forever to find a way out.

Chapter 2
I walk down the same street.
There is a deep hole in the sidewalk.
I pretend I don't see it.
I fall in again.
I can't believe I am in the same place.
But it isn't my fault.
It still takes a long time to get out.

Chapter 3
I walk down the same street.
There is a deep hole in the sidewalk.
I see it is there.
I still fall in ... it's a habit.
My eyes are open.
I know where I am.
It is my fault.
I get out immediately.

Chapter 4
I walk down the same street.
There is a deep hole in the sidewalk.
I walk around it.

Chapter 5
I walk down another street.

A dear friend—I'll call her Betty—dated a long line of emotionally unavailable men. When Betty began to take responsibility for her own life, she realized that she was the one attracting these men. With the help of a therapist she explored why. Betty began to realize that she was afraid of intimate relationships, more specifically she was afraid of becoming vulnerable and being rejected. Dating men who were emotionally unavailable was safe since the relationships rarely progressed to the point that she would have to reveal herself. Further, Betty realized that she was attracting men like her father. When Betty was a child, her dad had traveled for his work and wasn't around much. And when he was at home, he wasn't emotionally available.

After reviewing my past relationships, I found a pattern of attracting men who were not as financially sound as I am. I realized that this was due, in part, to a false belief that I was not loveable as I am. *Why would someone want to be with me? If he knew who I really am, he'll run.* As I dug deeper, I learned the inequality of our financial situations was related to power. To guard against feeling powerless, as I did with my father, I attracted men who did not have the financial resources that I had. While I said I wanted an equal partner, it was obvious that I wanted anything but.

Jung once wrote: "Where love reigns, there is no will to power; and where the will to power is paramount, love is lacking." And James Hollis writes in *On This Journey We Call Life:* "Only through considerable self-knowledge can we make a different choice and change the course of our relational history. Taking responsibility for doing this work is in fact the best way we can love the other." Once I became aware of my "power of the purse pattern," I was able to break it and attract Don, who is on similar financial footing as I am.

Finally, it's important to reclaim the projections we place on potential partners. Whether we are conscious of it or not, all of us have an ideal partner profile. We have a list of physical, mental, emotional, and spiritual characteristics that we seek in a potential partner. Before I met Don I committed my ideal partner profile to paper. My list included such attributes as spiritual, kind, gentle, considerate, and smart. Then I went about the work of ensuring that I myself met the characteristics on that list. Almost all the self-help books agree that the first step in attracting a potential mate is to catalog all these characteristics in a list, but then most self-help books neglect to mention the next important step: review that list and see if we match all the characteristics we are seeking. If not, we have some work to do.

Timing Is Everything

It was not until six years after we first met that Don and I began dating seriously. Do you remember the story about Jake McCord, the Georgia folk artist? Jake used to place pieces of his art in the yard to "season." When collectors would visit and try to buy one of the yard pieces, he would emphatically say, "It ain't ready yet." Don and I weren't ready yet. Sometimes it takes a while to find the right spiritual partner. When this happens we are called to practice patience, trust in a divine order, and surrender to God's will. In the meantime, we can prepare for love by reviewing past patterns, reclaiming our projections, and seeking friends who can become spiritual partners.

We've covered quite a bit in this section. We learned spiritual partnerships are relationships between equals for the purpose of spiritual growth. I suggested spiritual partnerships are a kind of graduate program for the soul, and the three paths are our curriculum. We saw that while spiritual partners can be friends or family, the spiritual partnerships that provide the greatest growth opportunities are those with romantic partners. I reviewed six components of spiritual partnerships, and we discussed six truths about spiritual partners as significant others. After a discussion about preparing for and attracting a spiritual partner, I suggested that there's a divine timing to entering into a spiritual relationship. Above all, we have to trust that when we are ready a partner will come.

CHAPTER FIFTY-THREE

Tools, Practices, and Questions

We've already covered many of the tools, exercises, and practices that would be helpful in attracting and retaining a romantic spiritual partner. To review, these include:
- Imago Therapy
- The Blueprint of We
- Reviewing, renegotiating, and renewing commitments
- Reviewing past patterns
- Reclaiming projections
- Attracting friends who are spiritual partners
- Writing an ideal relationship profile
- Packing for the journey

This last is a new tool that I particularly like. I'll describe it in the next section and will also include a list of questions for you to consider.

Packing for the Journey

Some years ago I stumbled on a book that changed the way I travel: *The Way of the Traveler: Making Every Trip a Journey of Self-Discovery* by Joseph Dispenza. Little did I know then that Joseph would become a dear friend, as well as a valued spiritual guide for me. In his book, Joseph offers a number of suggestions and practices that help make travel more intentional and inspirational. One of my favorites is writing down each attribute you'd like to take on your journey on an index card and packing them in your suitcase. If being in a spiritual partnership is a journey—which I believe it is—what attributes would I pack? Of course I'd include curiosity, commitment, courage, compassion, and conscious communication. I'd also want to pack respect, responsibility, humor, gratitude, and generosity. You may have noticed the absence of love from this list. For me it is a given. What about you? What attributes would—or will—you pack?

Questions

1. Looking over past relationships, can you find a pattern that may help you define your "Imago match"? For instance, are you attracted to rebels, bad boys or girls, or men or women who seem incapable of commitment?
2. Have you ever experienced a safe container? If so, describe your experience. If not, describe how you think a safe container would work.
3. What is the most important thing you can do to nurture a loving relationship? Think about people you know who are in good relationships. How do they demonstrate this quality, action, or trait?

SECTION VIII

Wrapping Up

A Country Fair for Those Mad with Love
Ramprasad

Drive me out of my mind, O Mother!
What use is esoteric knowledge
    Or philosophical knowledge
Transport me totally with the burning wine
Of your all-embracing love.
Mother of mystery, who imbues with mystery
    The hearts of those who love you,
Immerse me irretrievably
In the stormy ocean without boundary,
Pure love, pure love, pure love.
Wherever your lovers reside
    Appears like a madhouse
To common perception.
Some are laughing with your freedom,
Others weep tears of your tenderness,
Still others dance, whirling with your bliss.
Even your devoted Gautama, Moses,
Krishna, Jesus, Nanak and Muhammad
    Are lost in the rapture of pure love.
This poet stammers,

Overcome with longing:
'When? When? When?
When will I be granted companionship
    With her intense lovers?'
Their holy company is heavenly
A country fair for those mad with love
Where every distinction
Between master and disciple disappears
Their love of love sings:
'Mother! Mother! Mother!'
Who can fathom your mystery,
    Your eternal play of love with love?
You are divine madness, O goddess,
Your love the brilliant crown of madness,
Please make this poor poet madly wealthy
    With the infinite treasure of your love

The Big Burn

I love the great "Aha!" And there's nothing I like better than to log an insight into my journal. I do this not so much to celebrate the flash of insight, but to capture it. I'm so afraid that I'll forget it. Several years ago, I made the decision to burn all my journals as a symbolic gesture of letting go and trusting that I've received what knowledge I need. Friends offered their pasture to me for this ritual, and on a cold windless winter morning I burned more than forty journals dating back over ten years. Later that afternoon my friend returned to the fire pit to check on the cinders. The journals were all reduced to black ash…except one small sliver of charred paper. On it I had written: "I am ready."

CHAPTER FIFTY-FOUR

Revisit the Highlights

Let's review the highlights of all we've covered. We discussed how we long for "*the* One," even those of us in relationships, and how this longing is often misdirected. When we shift the object of our longing from "*the* One" to "*The* One," or the divine, everything shifts, and we begin to discover the "peace that passes all understanding."

Within each of us is a longing to be loved and to love unconditionally. This is a holy longing, since to give and receive unconditional love is the full expression of our divine self. Yet most of us project this longing onto a romantic partner, seeking perfect love from our partner who, like us, is imperfect. This leaves us disappointed, disillusioned, and unfulfilled.

We are constantly on a continuum between ego and essence. Most of us think we are our egos rather than recognizing the deeper, purer aspect of our being—including our highest and divine selves. As a result, many of us operate from our defended selves much of the time. The goal of essence is love. The opposite of love is not hate—it is fear.

The ego manipulates with fear, and our greatest fear is that we are unlovable as we are. This is largely due to childhood wounding. No matter how loving, accepting, and supportive our parents or primary caregivers were, they could not love us in the way we longed to be loved. They are human, and as such are imperfect and only capable of imperfect love.

Most of us are unconscious of this longing and project it out onto a potential or existing romantic partner in the hope, expectation, and need that "the One" will heal our childhood wounds and make us whole. We attract "Imago matches" who will wound us in similar ways our parents wounded us. When we remain unconscious to this, it only increases our frustration, disappointment, and longing.

The longing for this unconditional, perfect, or divine love can only be satiated by reunion and communion with the divine. If we follow longing home, it will lead us back to the divine—like the prodigal son who returns to the father. In order to come into reunion and communion with the divine, we must transcend the ego and connect with our essence, which is our divine self.

Unconditional love is the highest expression of the divine self. When we operate from essence rather than ego, we become channels of this divine or unconditional love. It flows through us fully and freely. Think of this love as an infinity symbol. The more we give this love, the more we receive it. The more we receive it, the more we give it. With each loop around the infinity symbol, our love expands until we recognize we are all one. This is the primary goal of essence. This is where all religions agree. This is what we call enlightenment. Put metaphorically, we come home. We return to the garden.

We are impatient. We crave an instant conversion experience. We hope to stumble on the burning bush, see Jesus' face in a teacup, or bump into him on the road to Damascus. Yet this doesn't happen for most of us. Enlightenment is a process, and it can take years, a lifetime, or many lifetimes to achieve. Yet along the way we get glimpses of our divine selves, unconditional love, and unity. We may experience them in a sunset, the birth of a child, the arms of our lover, or the rich beauty of stillness and silence. And these glimpses transform us.

Whether we are conscious of it or not, we are always moving toward enlightenment, or reunion and communion with the divine. There is a way, however, that we can move toward enlightenment more intentionally. We can follow our longing home. We do this by intentionally embarking on the three paths:

- Path One: The evolution from the unconscious to the conscious self. We become aware and know our self.
- Path Two: The evolution from the defended to the authentic self. We become the expression of our most authentic self.
- Path Three: The evolution from the higher to the divine self. We transcend ego to become our divine self, and we express that essence by giving and receiving unconditional love. It's here that all longing ceases.

We embark on these paths simultaneously, knowing that every person we meet and every situation we encounter can help us evolve. As we travel deeper and deeper down each path, we find that we are now ready to attract a special kind of relationship: a spiritual partnership in which each partner is dedicated to the other's spiritual growth. There is no better way for us to grow, heal, love, and strengthen our connection to our selves, all of creation, and divinity.

There are six components of spiritual partnerships:
1. Commitment
2. Courage
3. Compassion
4. Conscious Communication
5. Curiosity
6. Confrontation

Spiritual partnerships are safe containers. They welcome all parts of a person, known and unknown, comfortable and uncomfortable, spoken and unspoken. Spiritual partnerships take work, but the work is worth it. Sometimes spiritual partnerships dissolve. When they do, we attempt to leave them with at least as much consciousness and grace as when we created them.

In closing, as I reflect over the twenty plus years between the end of my marriage and my relationship with Don, I see a very important truth about relationships: as long as we blame fate for withholding a significant other who loves us deeply, we will be incapable of attracting the kind of relationship we truly want. It's not until we look within that we can attract a true spiritual partner. Instead of expecting—or demanding—that another meet our needs (most of which are based upon old childhood wounds), we take responsibility for our own healing. Instead of expecting that another love and approve of us unconditionally, we do that for ourselves. Instead of projecting our desire to be in union and communion with the divine or another, we pull our focus in and strengthen our own relationship with God.

Thank you for traveling this journey with me. It's been my privilege to walk with you if only for a short while. If you remember nothing else from our time together, I hope it's this: I feel your pain. I know what it's like to long for love so much that your bones hurt. But I also know what it's like to feel truly loved and to love truly. The distance between longing and love is not as great as you might imagine. Look out, and look within. Great love is coming. The time to prepare is now.

CHAPTER FIFTY-FIVE

Poem, Prayer, and Promise

Before we part ways, I'd like to leave you with a poem, a prayer, and a promise.

Love After Love
Derick Walcott

The time will come
when, with elation,
you will greet yourself arriving
at your own door, in your own mirror

and each will smile at the other's welcome,
and say, sit here. Eat.
You will love again the stranger who was your self.
Give wine. Give bread. Give back your heart
to itself, to the stranger who has loved you

all your life, whom you ignored
for another, who knows you by heart.
Take down the love letters from the bookshelf,

the photographs, the desperate notes,
peel your own image from the mirror.
Sit. Feast on your life.

Prayer
Creator, show us how to convert our longing into holy longing
So that we may experience that "peace that passes all understanding"
Where we are released from all expecting, anticipating, wanting, hoping, and scheming
Help us to know ourselves
So that we may become the full expression of all we are
Ready to heed your call home
To reunion and communion with you
And creator, help us to recognize our divinity
And the divinity that lives in all people
So that we may see that we are all creations of you
And as such, we are one family and one energy
United
Perfect
Worthy of love
And finally, Creator, when we are ready
Unite us with a partner with whom we can grow spiritually,
Come to know our true nature,
And become closer with you.

Amen

Promise
We are stardust; we are golden.
We are billion year-old carbon.
And we've got to get ourselves back to the Garden

"Woodstock"
Singer-Songwriter Joni Mitchell

Is it really possible to shed the suffering of separation and share in the sweetness, peace, and harmony of your connectedness? Can you really feel healthy, happy, and whole? Can you cease all longing and bask in the arms of unconditional love? Absolutely! You can return to the garden. You're already on your way.

May I Ask You a Favor?

Help me spread the word. If you found this book of value, please write a favorable review on Amazon.com and Goodreads.com. Also, consider recommending or passing this book onto a friend.

Going Deeper

Books

Almaas, A. H. *The Unfolding Now: Realizing Your True Nature Through the Practice of Presence.* Boston: Shambhala, 2008.

Bach, Tara, Ph.D. *Radical Acceptance: Embracing Your Life with the Heart of a Buddha.* New York: Bantam, 2003.

Blanton, Brad. Ph.D. *Radical Honesty: How to Transform Your Life By Telling the Truth.* New York: Dell Publishing, 1994.

Bradshaw, John. *Homecoming: Reclaiming and Championing Your Inner Child.* New York: Bantam, 1990.

Brown, Brené. *Daring Greatly: How the Courage to Be Vulnerable Transforms the Way We Live, Love, Parent, and Lead.* New York: Avery, 2015.

Brunton, Paul. *The Short Path to Enlightenment: Instructions for Immediate Awakening.* Burdett, New York: Larson Publishers, 2014.

Cameron, Julia. *The Right to Write: An Invitation and Initiation into the Writing Life.* New York: Jeremy P. Tarcher/Putnam, 1998.

Cope, Stephen. *Yoga and the Quest for the True Self.* New York: Bantam, 2000.

Dispenza, Joseph. *The Way of the Traveler: Making Every Trip a Journey of Self-Discovery.* Emeryville, CA: Avalon Travel Publishing, Inc., 2002.

Dyer, Wayne. *The Power of Intention: Learning to Co-create Your World Your Way.* Carlsbad, CA: Hay House, Inc., 2004.

Elkins, David, N. Ph.D. *Beyond Religion: Eight Alternative Paths to the Sacred.* Wheaton, IL: The Theosophical Publishing House, 1998.

Emoto, Masaru. *The Hidden Messages in Water.* Hillsboro, OR: Beyond Words Publishing, Inc., 2004.

Ferrini, Paul. *Dancing with the Beloved: Opening Our Hearts to the Lesson of Love.* Greenfield, MA: Heartways Press, 2001.

———. *Embracing Our True Self: A New Paradigm Approach to Healing Our Wounds, Finding Our Gifts, and Fulfilling Our Spiritual Purpose.* Greenfield, MA: Heartways Press, 2007.

———. *I Am the Door: Exploring the Christ Within.* Greenfield, MA: Heartways Press, 1999.

———. *Return to the Garden: Reflections of the Christ Mind, Part IV.* Greenfield, MA: Heartways Press, 1998.

Ferrucci, Piero. *The Power of Kindness: The Unexpected Benefits of Leading a Compassionate Life.* New York: Jeremy P. Tarcher/Putnam Book, 2006.

Ford, Arielle. *Wabi Sabi Love: The Ancient Art of Finding Perfect Love in Imperfect Relationships.* New York: HarperCollins, 2012.

Ford, Debbie. *The Right Questions: Ten Essential Questions to Guide You to an Extraordinary Life.* New York: HarperCollins, 2004.

Goldberg, Whoopi. *If Someone Says "You Complete Me," RUN!: Whoopi's Big Book of Relationships.* New York: Hatchette Books, 2015.

Goldman, Daniel. *Emotional Intelligence: Why It Can Matter More Than IQ.* New York: Bantam Dell, 1996.

Harris, Bud, Ph.D. *Sacred Selfishness: A Guide to Living a Life of Substance.* Maui, HI: Inner Ocean Publishing, 2002.

Hendrix, Harville, Ph.D. *Getting the Love You Want: A Guide for Couples.* New York: Harper & Row Publishers, Inc., 1988.

Hollis, James. *On This Journey We Call Our Life: Living the Questions.* Toronto, ON: Inner City Books, 2003.

———. *The Eden Project: In Search of the Magical Other.* Toronto, ON: Inner City Books, 1998.

Howard, Vernon. *The Power of the Supermind.* Pine, AZ: New Life Foundation, 2011.

Hudson, Russ, and Don Richard Riso. *The Wisdom of the Enneagram: The Complete Guide to Psychological and Spiritual Growth for the Nine Personality Types.* New York: Bantam Books, 1990.

Johnson, Robert. A. *Inner Work: Using Dreams and Active Imagination for Personal Growth.* San Francisco: Harper, 1986.

Johnson, Sue. *Hold Me Tight: Seven Conversations for a Lifetime of Love.* New York: Little, Brown, and Company, 2008.

Kingma, Daphne Rose. *The Future of Love.* New York: Doubleday, 1998.

———. *The Ten Things to Do When Your Life Falls Apart: An Emotional and Spiritual Handbook.* Novato, California: New World Library, 2010.

———. *When You Think You're Not Enough: The Four Life-Changing Steps to Loving Yourself.* San Francisco, Conari Press, 2012.

Lesser, Elizabeth. *Broken Open: How Difficult Times Can Help Us Grow.* New York: Villard Books, 2004.

———. *The Seeker's Guide: Making Your Life a Spiritual Adventure.* New York: Villard Books, 1999.

Moss, Richard, MD. *The Mandala of Being: Discovering the Power of Awareness.* Novato, CA: New World Library, 2007.

O'Donohue, John. *Beauty: The Invisible Embrace: Rediscovering the True Sources of Compassion, Serenity, and Hope.* New York: HarperCollins, 2004.

Pierrakos, Eva. *The Pathwork of Self-Transformation.* New York: Bantam Books, 1990.

Pierrakos, Eva, and Judith Saly. *Creating Union: The Essence of Intimate Relationships.* Madison, VA, Pathwork Press, 2002.

Robbins, Tom. *Another Roadside Attraction.* New York: Bantam Dell, 1971.

———. *Still Life with Woodpecker.* New York: Bantam Dell, 1980.

———. *Tibetan Peach Pie: A True Account of an Imaginative Life.* New York: HarperCollins, 2014.

Rand, Ayn. *The Fountainhead.* New York: New American Library, 1943.

Siegel, Randy. *Engineer Your Career: Build Your Best Blueprint.* Asheville, NC: Wyngate Publishing, 2011.

———. *The Inspired Life: How Connection and Contribution Create Power, Passion, and Joy.* Asheville, NC: Wyngate Publishing: 2010.

Singer, Michael, A. *The Untethered Soul: The Journey Beyond Yourself.* Oakland, CA: New Harbinger Publications, Inc., 2007.

Thesenga, Susan. *The Undefended Self: Living the Pathwork of Spiritual Wholeness.* Madison, VA: Pathwork Press, 1994.

Tolle Eckhart. *A New Earth: Awakening to Your Life's Purpose.* New York: Plume, 2005.

———. *The Power of Now: A Guide to Spiritual Enlightenment.* Novato, CA: New World Library, 1999.

Triffet, Carrie. *Long Time No See: Diaries of an Unlikely Messenger.* Ventura, CA: Gentle Joyous Industries, 2014.

———. *The Enlightenment Project.* Ventura, CA: Gentle Joyous Industries, 2011.

Walsch, Neal Donald. *Conversations with God: An Uncommon Dialogue, Book One.* New York: G. P. Putnam's Sons, 1995.

Welwood, John. *Perfect Love, Imperfect Relationships: Healing the Wound of the Heart.* Boston, MA: Trumpeter Books, 2006.

Wilbur, Ken. *One Taste: Daily Reflections on Integral Spirituality.* Boston, MA: Shambhala Publications, Inc., 2000.

Williamson, Marianne. *A Return to Love: Reflections on the Principles of A Course of Miracles.* New York: HarperCollins Publishers, Inc., 1992.

———. *Enchanted Love: The Mystical Power of Intimate Relationships.* New York: Simon & Schuster: 2001.

Zukav, Gary. *The Seat of the Soul.* New York: Fireside, 1990.

Other Resources

Workshops: RandySiegelWrites.com
Occasionally Randy conducts workshops on the search for "The One" based upon the principles and practices presented in this book. If you or your group is interested in hosting a workshop, please contact Randy at Randy@RandySiegelWrites.com.

One-to-One Coaching: YourInternalGPS.com
If you would like to work with Randy individually, contact him through YourInternalGPS.com or RandySiegelWrites.com. Please note: he takes only a limited number of clients each month.

Blueprint of We: blueprintofwe.com
"The Blueprint of We" is a conscious contract between two people in relationship. It outlines personal preferences and expectations.

Enneagram: enneagraminstitute.com
The Enneagram is one of my favorite models for human psychology and spirituality. While there are many excellent books and websites on the subject, I especially like this site.

About Randy Siegel

Randy Siegel believes that love and work give us the greatest potential for growth because that's where our inner challenges are most visible. Since 1998, Siegel has inspired thousands of professions worldwide to "stand in their power by becoming the full expression of all they are" for such organizations as the Recording Academy (The Grammy Awards), State Farm Insurance, and the American Alliance of Museums.

Siegel has written five books including one on breakups: *Break Up, Wake Up, Move On: From Broken Heart to Open Heart, Prepare for the Partner You've Always Longed For.* He's written articles for *Balance Magazine*, the *Washington Post*, and other publications and is frequently quoted by the media. Siegel, his partner, Don, and their dog, Loodle the Poodle, divide their time between Asheville, North Carolina and Saint Simons Island, Georgia.

Connect with Randy on Facebook and his websites LinkToRandy.com and RandySiegelWrites.com. He'd love to stay in touch.

Other Books by Randy Siegel

Break up, Wake Up, Move On: Broken Heart to Open Heart; Prepare for the Partner You've Always Longed For

The Inspired Life: How Connection and Contribution Create Power, Passion, and Joy

Engineer Your Career: Package, Present, and Promote Yourself for Success

PowerHouse Presenting: Become the Communicator You Were Born to Be

All are available through Amazon.com.

www.ingramcontent.com/pod-product-compliance
Lightning Source LLC
Chambersburg PA
CBHW070608300426
44113CB00010B/1458